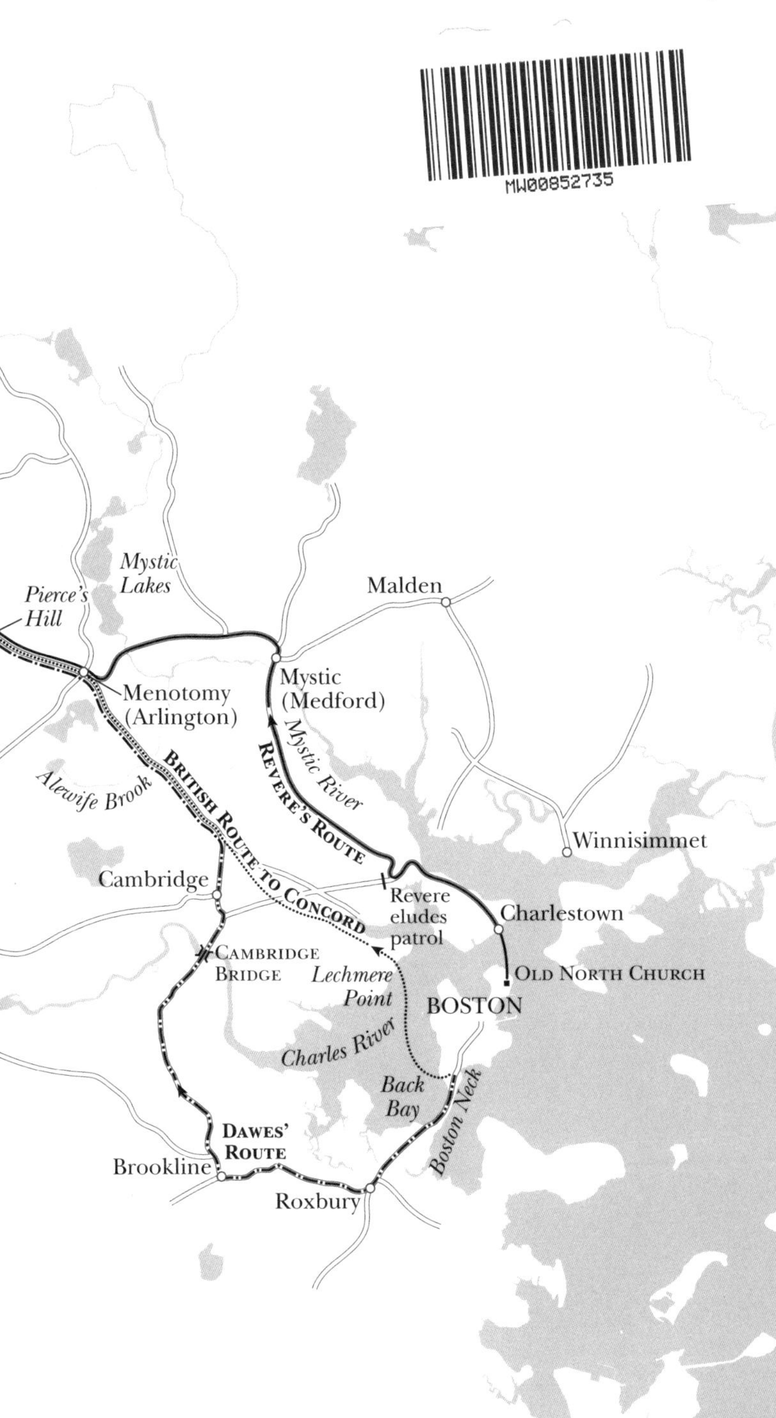
MW00852735
Pierce's Hill
Mystic Lakes
Malden
Menotomy (Arlington)
Mystic (Medford)
Mystic River
Revere's Route
British Route to Concord
Alewife Brook
Winnisimmet
Cambridge
Revere eludes patrol
Charlestown
Cambridge Bridge
Lechmere Point
Old North Church
BOSTON
Charles River
Back Bay
Boston Neck
Dawes' Route
Brookline
Roxbury

The RIDE

PAUL REVERE *and the* NIGHT THAT SAVED AMERICA

KOSTYA KENNEDY

ST. MARTIN'S PRESS
NEW YORK

First published in the United States by St. Martin's Press, an imprint of St. Martin's Publishing Group

Printed in the United States of America. For information, address St. Martin's Publishing Group, 120 Broadway, New York, NY 10271.

www.stmartins.com

Design by Meryl Sussman Levavi

Endpaper: National Park Service, public domain, via Wikimedia Commons.

The Library of Congress Cataloging-in-Publication Data is available upon request.

ISBN 9781250341372 (hardcover)
ISBN 9781250341389 (ebook)

First Edition: 2025

1 3 5 7 9 10 8 6 4 2

For Jeremy Boal

CONTENTS

The RIDE

April 18, 1775

I

ECHOES

WHAT IF THE MILITIAMEN HAD NOT BEEN WAITing at the Lexington Green at dawn on that April day in 1775, to test and slow the British? What if they had not then been at Concord a few hours later, 220 strong, ready and resolute on the high ground?

Those Patriot soldiers arrived by the hundreds that morning, then by the thousands, armed and keen and strengthened in their numbers. They mustered on the damp, open fields and on the forest edges along the Old Concord Road. Farmers and tradesmen, with their muskets and fowling pieces in hand. They turned back the redcoats and then fired on them in their retreat, routing them out of town and back off the land that the Patriots knew now as their own. Villagers from the highlands and the low, ministers and deists and nonbelievers, men dressed in whatever clothes they had—their patched and varied breeches, their worn straight-last boots—a hodgepodge of an earnest crew transformed by necessity and determination into American soldiers who that morning showed the will that would drive them in the weeks and months ahead, the will that would win the Revolutionary War.

Suppose they had not come that morning after all, suppose they had not been so timely in their arrival, not been so committed to their call?

Suppose instead the seasoned British soldiers, in their fine cocked hats and under their generals' command, had in their ransacking of Concord's Barrett Farm found and taken the stores of gunpowder and ammunition they had come to seize. Imagine if the British had caught the Americans by surprise, as they'd intended. Imagine if, in Lexington, they had killed or captured Samuel Adams or John Hancock, delivering on the bounty that had been put on those men by the king. What would have happened to the path of the American Revolution then?

If not for that first morning of battle—of impudent, plucky, stunning, and world-shifting Patriot success—

would the rebelling American army have continued to mobilize so confidently? Would it have stayed so unified in the face of defeat and death, have remained so emboldened to succeed? Would the army have fared so well (even in defeat) in the Battle of Bunker Hill, eight weeks later? Would the Revolution have unfolded so quickly as it did? Would we have July 4, 1776, as our Day of Independence? Or how much longer might the British have held their grip? Into the 1780s, the 1790s, the 1800s, and beyond? And if they had held that longer grip, what might then have been the implications for the establishment and growth of the American democracy in the years and decades that followed? What would be the implications today?

When we ask these things, when we consider the plausible alternatives to the chain of events that occurred on April 18 and April 19, 1775, we are asking this: What might have happened, how might the much-documented and much-deconstructed birth of our nation have unfolded, and with what repercussions, had not Paul Revere mounted his borrowed horse and set out to ride those critical miles in those critical hours across the simmering moonlit land, to rouse the countryside and deliver the news? What would have become of the Revolution, of its crucial early days? What would have become of the whole hard, taxing, extraordinary journey to independence, if not for Paul Revere and his midnight ride?

* * *

Of all the Revolutionary War events that live on in collective memory—immortalized in art and prose—perhaps none conjures such a succinct image as Paul Revere galloping on his horse under cover of darkness, warning of the British threat. Perhaps no night was more critical to our fate.

If the Ride echoes in romance through the imperishable Henry Wadsworth Longfellow verse that for generations of Americans served as history, it remains resonant for its immediacy, its example of courage and enterprise and urgency. The story endures because of what it represents and what it was. Ordinary men meeting the moment of their lives. An engraver in Paul Revere, a tanner in William Dawes, a doctor in Samuel Prescott, and a network of some forty riders then coursing through the countryside, spreading word of what was at hand. Longfellow's poem, written eighty-five years after the fact, is not bound by strict accuracy or obligation to detail—significantly, there were the other riders, too—yet the poem remains steeped in truth: a man riding horseback through the late-night hours on a fervent mission to save a nation in its embryonic, even pre-embryonic, state. It was Revere at the start and center of it all. It was Revere, booted and spurred, who raised the resistance, who helped to deliver the first, fateful stand.

He was forty years old and stood better than five feet, ten inches tall in his riding boots, taller, if only slightly, than most of the men around him. Broad across the chest and shoulders, burly. His hands were roughened from the work he did and roughened, too, from so often clutching the reins. Standing now on the far bank of the Charles, Revere could see the shape of the *Somerset,* the great British warship docked in the river—her masts rising in silhouette, her bobbing hull and readied gun decks a massive chiaroscuro under the night sky. Revere could feel the wet earth beneath his feet and the warmth off the mare's body as he put a hand against her side. The deacon's mare. "A very good horse," Revere would say. The hint of bowleggedness that may have attended Revere's gait in his daily life, the hitch and hint of a limp, all of that disappeared when he climbed onto the back of a horse. No one among the Sons of Liberty was a better, or more reliable, rider than Paul Revere.

He had, in the last days of 1773, ridden swiftly along the wintry Post Road the twelvescore miles from Boston to New York City to deliver, as he called it, an "account of the destruction of the tea"—the seminal event that had so powerfully churned the spirit of rebellion along the docks and waters of Boston Harbor. Revere had ridden that Post Road route again in the late summer and early fall of 1774, following the stone mile markers to New York and then continuing, still farther south, to Philadelphia, a 350-mile journey in all, to arrive at the First Continental Congress carrying dispatches from the selectmen of Boston. He had made a northward ride as well that year, more than sixty miles through a hard December wind on a failing horse, to arrive at Portsmouth, New Hampshire, and there pass along intelligence that led the Patriots to ambush the Royal watchmen and seize the powder at Fort William and Mary, fortifying themselves for the battles ahead. Revere rode missions at other times and to other places as well. When the movement needed a message delivered faithfully and without delay, Revere was the man to deliver it.

Now, it was the spring of 1775, warm for mid-April, and the white moon was already up in the clear, star-strewn sky, and the village roads and the country roads were quiet. At least seemingly so, for the moment. Rain had fallen that afternoon, big drops and then a misting before it cleared. It had rained the day before as well. Revere was preparing to set out on another ride, a much shorter ride than the earlier journeys, more pressing and less precise. He traveled light and bore no documents to support a message or directive—only his voice and what he knew. Revere had thirteen miles ahead of him on the first leg that night, maybe thirteen and a half. He might meet Dawes as he neared Lexington, he suspected. He would get to Adams and Hancock whatever the cost.

Revere stood for a moment on the muddy ground,

the Old North Church tall across the river before him, the mare, Brown Beauty, shifting on her hooves. Revere understood that for himself and for the others who might ride on this night—along close wooded paths and over wet meadows to visit the farmhouses and boarding-houses and homesteads, to sound the warning and make the appeal—this was the most important horseback ride of his life. The Regulars were out. The Royal Army was on the move.

Bell No. 6, a treble bell, at Old North Church

2

THE BELL RINGER, 1750

AS A YOUNG MAN LIVING IN THE NORTH END of Boston Paul Revere got himself a job as a bell ringer, a change ringer to be precise, sounding the church bells in the same way that bells were sounded in churches across the English countryside, a many-toned, overlapping rhythmic sound, a small well-ordered symphony. Revere was fifteen years old and the bell-ringing job was at the Old North Church, Christ Church, overlooking the shore from where boats pushed off toward Charlestown, across the waterway north of Boston.

This was in 1750, and the men and women of the colonies, those whose families had been there for generations and those who had recently come from England or elsewhere, were living together and alongside one another, under the authority of the Crown. Relations with the indigenous people were calm and cooperative in the area around Boston at this time. The French and Indian War, which would enlist Revere and so many other young men, and which would thunder for nine years through Canada and the western sweep of the colonies, had not yet begun.

Change ringing is a particular endeavor, a learned skill that came over to the colonies from England, where it began in the seventeenth century. In this kind of church-bell ringing a group of ringers, maybe as many as sixteen and rarely fewer than six, stand in a circle, each with a rope in his or her hands. Each bell is rung in succession, according to a precise preestablished pattern or sometimes as instructed by a leader, who calls out the order of ringing in real time. The Old North Church featured a peal of eight bells. They had been cast in Gloucester, England, by Abel Rudhall, whose father, Abraham, established the bell-casting company Rudhall of Gloucester in the 1680s, nearly seven decades before. Men had been founding bells in Gloucester since the 1200s, at least. One of the bells in the Old North Church bore—and still bears today—the inscription *We are the first ring of bells cast for the British Empire in North America, A.R. 1744.*

Each bell in the Old North belfry was, and is, affixed to a wooden wheel. From the wheel hangs the rope, maybe twenty-five feet down and through two ceilings and into the bell ringers' room. The smallest and lightest of the bells at Old North Church, the treble, weighs 620 pounds, and the heaviest bell, the tenor, weighs 1,545 pounds. Yet a change ringer does not need to be unusually strong. Gravity does most of the work. The bell starts in a mouth-up position, and as it gets swung around full circle to a stop, the clapper hits the sound bow just as the mouth faces outward from the belfry. From Old North Church the bells rang out loudly and splendidly for miles. They could be heard down around Beacon Hill, and over in Cambridge on the campus of Harvard, and up into Charlestown and out by the docks at Long Wharf. When Revere and the others rang the bells on a clear evening, the greater part of Boston heard a kind of waterfall of sound, a pattern full of discernible individual notes that then ran into the next.

Revere was one of a group of seven change ringers who signed on with the Old North Church, all of them boys about his age. The boys drew up a document after landing the job, a document that was as much a covenant among themselves as it was a contract with the church.

The boys referred to themselves as a society that would "not exceed eight persons" and pledged to ring at Old North Church at least one evening a week for a year. "None shall be admitted a member of this society without a unanimous vote of the members," the covenant said. It also specified that none of the undersigned would beg money from anyone at the church, and that they all were committed to ring at any time that the warden at Old North Church desired. The document was signed in this order and in this way:

John Dyer
Paul Revere
Josiah Flagg
Barthw Ballard
Jonathan Law
Jona. Brown junr,
Joseph Snelling

The boys had learned penmanship at the North Writing School, and several of them accented their signatures with flourishes, none larger than Revere's—a flashy, looping sweep beneath his name, a marking that, as he aged, he shed.

Likely one of these boys, not Revere, knew something of the craft of change-bell ringing. It's not so difficult to get a handle on it, but the practice requires a certain touch, as well as some specific knowledge and understanding and the memorizing of various patterns. Most typically it is a skill passed down. One of the boys' fathers or grandfathers may himself have been a bell ringer in England. As best as anyone can tell, Paul Revere and the rest of them were the first people to ring those bells, or any kind of changing bells, on American soil.

THE REVERE FAMILY didn't attend the Old North Church, which was an Episcopalian church. But rather they went regularly to the New Brick Church, a Congregationalist church. That was where Paul was baptized, and the church that his father and mother supported. Revere's father had come to Boston from France in 1715 when he was thirteen years old, and some years later he changed his name from Apollos Rivoire to Paul Revere, well before naming his firstborn son the same. The older Paul Revere believed in the simple Puritan ethic espoused at New Brick Church, in the importance of good, simple hard work and an uncompromising God.

North Writing was the most heavily attended school in Boston, and one where instructors prepared students for literate lives as artisans or tradesmen, though it was not the school with the greatest emphasis on book learning. By age fifteen the younger Paul Revere, our Paul as it were, was already learning the ways of his father's silversmithing business and of the importance of earning a living. His father did not subscribe to the religious perspective and structure of the Old North Church, but found nothing at all wrong with Paul getting a job there that paid.

The Reveres lived on Fish Street, which had earlier been known as the "common way by the water." Joshua Gee, a minister at New Brick Church, also lived on Fish Street, a few houses away. You could smell the ocean, and the incoming fruit of the sea, the good and the bad of it, from many streets in North Boston but perhaps nowhere more pungently than on Fish Street. The Reveres' home, and the silversmithing business, sat right by Clark's Wharf, where hauls of fish came in (and dead fish inevitably bobbed in the waters) along with innumerable other goods that were often unloaded all throughout the day.

To walk to the Old North Church from Fish Street would take Paul less than five minutes, barely three minutes when he hustled. Inside, he and the other boys climbed the gently curving staircase—twenty-four steps—to reach the balcony seating area in front of the organ. Then they would slip in behind the organ, moving sideways through a narrow passageway, and into the bell ringers' room, where the ropes hung and where the boys would ring according to the patterns, or methods, that the leader of the group set forth.

For any number of reasons the context and details around Revere's time as a bell ringer feel significant in the light of what he would go on to do with his life and what he would be remembered for. The boys showed real enterprise in finding, or in effect creating, the change-ringing job. Then they formed a responsible community complete with a kind of elder in John Dyer.

With Josiah Flagg, who was younger than Revere by two years, Revere would keep a friendship into adulthood. In 1764 Revere engraved and helped publish a book of psalms that Flagg had collected and written down. Revere and Flagg knew each other through the smallpox fears, and in the late 1760s they would convene along with others at the Liberty Tree to protest the tyranny of British rule. Joseph Snelling also remained connected to Revere's life. Some among this small group of teenage bell ringers were people Revere would still know a quarter century later, in the spring of 1775.

Revere had a fondness for the rules and accountabilities of such voluntary societies as the bell ringers. He would go on to belong to many of them, most significantly the Masons, who were integral to the devising and organizing of the early acts of resistance to British rule and who were equally integral to the maintenance of trust and understanding among its members when events were engineered and then unfolded in the preamble and onset of the Revolutionary War.

It was still later in his life, in 1792, when Paul Revere was no longer in the thick of things, when he was fifty-seven years old and still as industrious as any man, that he embarked on a business casting church bells, the very first church bells cast in America. Revere's earliest bells gave a crude, unpolished sound, but over time the bells he cast would become known for their excellence of shape and for the clear, high quality of their peal. Revere and his son Joseph Warren Revere oversaw the casting of hundreds of bells during the later years of Paul's life. Scores of them still ring from church belfries in New England towns and villages today.

The ringing of the bells at the Old North Church during the time of Paul Revere's childhood had various meanings. The boys rang to signify the end of Sunday services and the nearing of the Sunday meal. They rang to announce a wedding or a birth or to honor a notable death. The bells sounded over the streets where the boys and their families lived, and the shops where they worked and the waters where they would sometimes swim. Ringing a bell like this was, finally, a means to alert people to something happening, to summon them to a place and to engage them in a common thought, to get the message out, to let them know that there was a reason to prepare themselves, to gather and to act.

The Green Dragon Tavern

3

KINSHIP

In the years after Paul Revere's father died, and after Revere had fought a grueling and anonymous turn with the British army against French forces in the French and Indian War, in the years when he and Sarah were newly married and their first children were born, he joined the Ancient Order of Masons, the Freemasons, and began to sharpen his view of the world and the situation around him and to determine his own aspirations. The Masons met on the first floor of the Green Dragon Tavern, on Union Street by the working shores of Mill Pond.

The members sat at long tables, and in rows of chairs, and when the meetings ended and you stepped out into the night, you could smell the salted air and the day's labor coming in off the pond. In summers the Masons gathered once a month from 6:00 P.M. until 10:00 P.M. In winters it was five until nine.

Paul's father had died suddenly, at age fifty-one, when Paul was nineteen. He was buried under a stone marker in the Old Granary grounds surrounded by the graves of his wife's family, the Hitchbourns. Apollos Rivoire had journeyed to America from a tiny, landlocked town in the southwest of France, arriving alone to the Boston docks at age thirteen, with that French name, and a French accent. He apprenticed to a silversmith and then set up a shop of his own and changed his name to Revere and advertised his work in the newspapers. He married an American woman and attended the New Brick Church, to which he gave at a level above his means. Upon his death he left behind his hardworking, can-do example and bequeathed to his son Paul, the second of nine children and the eldest boy, the silversmithing business. Paul had been his father's apprentice, and after the death he had to learn the last points of the trade on his own. A few years after he had begun to run the business professionally, Paul, at age twenty-five, came to the Masons, in part as a way to meet new people and to grow his clientele.

The masons of the Middle Ages designed and built

great structures: cathedrals, castles, monasteries. They were specialists, skilled and sought after, and often they traveled straight from one job to the next. In a spirit of professional collegiality, the masons formed an order, a fraternity, that began to convene at lodges in England and Scotland. Over the decades the talk and activities at the lodges expanded beyond the challenges of stonework and evolved into a social order that provided, along with comradery, a kind of moral instruction and guidance. Beginning in the 1600s and certainly by the 1700s, the requirement, or even the expectation, that the members of the order would work in masonry disappeared.

Masonic lodges were authorized by the Grand Lodges in the United Kingdom and had operated in the colonies, in Boston and Philadelphia, since before Revere was born. The new St. Andrew's Lodge, to which Revere was in 1760 an early initiate, had been established in dissent—a workingman's alternative to the more elite, more moneyed St. John's Lodge, most of whose members (though not all) were loyal to the Crown.

The members of St. Andrew's worked as boatbuilders and sailmakers, shipwrights, gunsmiths, coopers, and painters. By and large they were men (and only men) who used their hands and who depended on a healthy maritime economy, a good flow of commerce through the ports. During meetings at the Green Dragon Tavern the lodge members discussed matters of internal governance and external industry, and they abided by clear, stated values—the most critical being that you broke no oath, and that you acted toward the benefit of your Masonic brother and to the benefit of your fellow man and woman. It was at the lodge that Revere formed alliances across the artisan and mechanic communities and where he built a strong and respected position among the men who plied those trades. The Green Dragon Tavern sat less than a quarter of a mile from where Revere lived and worked.

Like most of his fellow St. Andrew's Masons Revere was without a deep education. He had no connection then to politics, no claim to any agency beyond the parameters of his own career and life. He was nearing thirty, thickset and purposeful in manner. Likable and reliable. Ambitious, practical, hale.

At St. Andrew's, members attained organizational status through active participation and committed effort. Revere proved unrestrained in his appetite for work and community. Over the years at St. Andrew's through the 1760s and into the 1770s, he rose swiftly through the Masonic hierarchy: apprentice, junior deacon, junior warden, senior warden, secretary, master. He was part of a committee that handled St. Andrew's purchase of the Green Dragon Tavern. He sat on a committee that wrote to Scotland to resolve some matters relating to St. Andrew's charter. For several years Revere helped arrange and execute the lodge's annual summer feast of John the

Baptist. He drew up procedural regulations for members' funerals, and he drew up regulations for the dispensing of charity. He was among those members of St. Andrew's who signed bylaws that forbade swearing during meetings and that determined that members could not be "disguised in liquor." Revere was active across a range of duties, and he showed up. According to *Paul Revere and Freemasonry,* a 1985 book by Edith Steblecki, Revere attended 169 of 185 Masonic meetings between 1761 and 1771. The goings-on and discussions at St. Andrew's were closely held and operated in an environment dependent upon internal secrets and codes. The Masons were good at planning things, and they took care of their own.

Deep friendships formed at St. Andrew's. So did a collective spirit, a tendency toward rebellion and independence that simmered even in the years when the relationship with the Crown was in the main untroubled. That rebellious tendency came to a boil through the developments that ultimately kindled the flame for revolution: the Stamp Act of 1765, which the Crown imposed with the intention of collecting a tax on the paper the colonists used, and then the Townshend Acts of 1767, which levied a tax on imports of glass, lead, and tea. The Stamp Act was soon abolished, but the suggestion of it, the insult as many colonists felt it, had been permanently lodged. Greater unrest—letters of defiance, protests on the streets—followed the Townshend Acts, which is why, in October of 1768, four thousand British troops came ashore at the Boston docks to occupy and attempt to control the city.

Some of the troops would return home after a while, replaced by other British soldiers. Some troops deserted and began a civilian or military life among the Patriots. Some troops simply stayed on and rose in rank and never left. For the people of Boston an uncomfortable feeling touched their daily lives, a feeling that stayed with them as the months and then the years went on, the sense of being intruded upon, of being under watch.

On the night of December 16, 1773, a Thursday five years after those troops docked in Boston Harbor, attendance at the Masonic meeting proved unusually sparse. Many of the members, Revere included, were at that precise time in painted face climbing aboard British ships anchored at Griffin's Wharf—the *Beaver,* the *Dartmouth,* and the *Eleanor*—to protest the Crown's enforced taxes by relieving those ships of 340 chests, that is, an extraordinary forty-six tons, of black tea.

By then St. Andrew's had evolved its charter, earning the designation Massachusetts Grand Lodge. The threescore, then fourscore, members of St. Andrew's Lodge were hardly alone in their resistance to British control. They were a fraction of the many resisters in the city and in the outlying towns. Yet the lodge and its members became a vital force for thought, organization, and resolve. Along with the many tradesmen who came to St. Andrew's, and along with the familiar friends to Paul Revere—his cousin, the boatbuilder Nathaniel Hitchborn, Revere's childhood friend, now jeweler, Josiah Flagg, and others—arrived a young physician. He was Harvard educated, keen for action, and marked by intelligence, charm, and a talent for public speaking that he used to declaim upon the Stamp Act and the Townshend Acts and to help inspire the colonists in their response. Revere first met the young doctor at St. Andrew's in 1761, and a few years after that a bond took hold. Over time, and in the context of the events that would define Revere in life and in death—events that would define the onset of the Revolutionary War—that doctor became as critical and influential a friend as Paul Revere ever had: Dr. Joseph Warren.

LATER, REVERE WOULD think back on Warren. After the fateful days and weeks of 1775, after Warren had fallen at the Battle of Bunker Hill and later still after he, Revere, had been called upon to identify Warren's remains, Revere would recall how much Warren had meant to his life. Through the years Warren had helped shape Revere's views and his approach to the resistance. Warren, perhaps more than anyone else, had led Revere to his role and purpose as an express rider. And it was Warren who, upon learning that the Royal Army was on the move on the night of April 18, 1775, directed Revere and William Dawes on the routes they should ride out of Boston, to Lexington.

There was a gestural elegance to Warren, a fluidity to his limbs, a firmness to his trunk. He bore a fierce, unbending courage in words and deeds. By the time of Bunker Hill, June 17, 1775, Warren had been named a major general of the fledgling army, but he chose instead to fight alongside the common soldiers of the militia, and to fight to the very last of the British assault even as others among the Patriots began the retreat. He took a musket ball between his eyes and was tossed by the redcoats into a shallow grave. Two years later Revere named his newborn son Joseph Warren Revere.

Warren had received his early schooling at Roxbury Latin—religion, literature, the classics. He graduated from Harvard with honors at seventeen, completed his medical degree by twenty-two. He showed his learning in his eloquence, in his orations and his writings against British taxation and rule. In the *Boston Gazette,* his words appeared under the signature A True Patriot. He also conveyed a confidence and unforced humility gained by being raised on a working farm. Warren was highly capable and eminently resourceful. A story about Warren from his days at Harvard followed him in his professional life. Some Harvard students had convened behind barred doors. Warren, wanting in, went to the roof of the house, shinnied down a spout, and swung into the meeting through a window. Just as he did, the spout snapped off and crashed to the ground. Warren glanced down at the fallen spout that might have brought him to a violent end, shrugged, then joined the discussion.

In his early days as a physician, Warren learned to deliver anesthesia, to perform surgery, and to suture wounds. He gave inoculations during the outbreak of smallpox in 1764. Warren treated patients of wealth and political power. He treated enslaved men and women. He treated laborers. He treated prominent Patriots and he treated redcoats eternally loyal to the Crown. Dr. Warren began to emerge as a known figure, a young doctor in demand.

Warren was twenty-three years old when he began to regularly attend and contribute to Masonic meetings. Eventually he would ascend to grand master. Though he was six years younger than Revere, a special kinship developed between them, a kinship beyond that which bound so many of the Masons at St. Andrew's. Revere and Warren, as teenagers, had each endured the sudden death of his father. Later, in the spring of 1773, Warren's and Revere's wives would die within days of each other. In their temperaments, too, there was a kinship. They shared an edge, an eagerness, and a curiosity. They forged their ways and pursued new ventures. In the years after the men of St. Andrew's had helped to throw the tea into Boston Harbor, a song of reminiscence could be heard on the streets, "The Rallying Song of the Tea Party." It included the passage:

Then rally, boys, and hasten on / To meet our chiefs at the Green Dragon. / Our Warren's there and bold Revere, / With hands to do and words to cheer.

Along with his silversmith business, Revere in the 1760s took on work as an engraver, making portraits and scenic representations, engraving the title page for a book of songs, and then a book of hymns, collected by Josiah Flagg. Revere also engraved a depiction of the royal warships moored in the harbor on the day in 1768 that the troops came ashore to take over Boston, and he accented this depiction with satirical text demeaning to the Crown's intent. Revere engraved other drawings with political sentiments, invariably amplifying Britain's tyranny as well as America's ideals. After the 1770 confrontation that became known as the Boston Massacre—the downtown altercation in which a small group of British soldiers fired on a hot, swarming civilian mob of colonists, killing five—Revere engraved a rendering of the scene by the painter Henry Pelham and quickly set it out for sale. The portrayal, to this day Revere's most famous work as well as the surviving representation of the event, was intentionally drawn to further villainize the British soldiers, showing them in a line with guns raised, a seemingly organized assault. The Patriots lie fallen, and there is no sense of how outnumbered the redcoats were, a bit of spin and propaganda meant to rouse anger against the British and support for the rebel cause, which it did.

All during those years Joseph Warren was writing and speaking out and rallying in condemnation of the British ministry. He had fallen in with the Whig leaders Samuel Adams and John Hancock and had become a partner to their design. It was Warren who delivered the most stirring public orations on the anniversaries of the Boston Massacre, standing at the site of it, on Congress and State. "May our land be a land of liberty, the seat of virtue, the asylum of the oppressed, a name and praise in the whole earth, until the last shock of time shall bury the empires of the world," Warren intoned at the commemoration in 1772.

At the 1775 anniversary, Warren stood in the same spot and again addressed the crowd. "The tools of power, in every age, have racked their inventions to justify the few in sporting with the happiness of the many," he said, and added, "The attempt of the British Parliament to raise a revenue from America, and our denial of their right to do it, have excited an almost universal inquiry into the rights of mankind in general." This was March 6, 1775, forty-three days before the night the British Regulars went to Lexington. "Our country is in danger," Warren exclaimed, "but not to be despaired of."

In the late 1760s, Revere, as another way to supplement his income, had studied and then taken up dentistry. He learned to clean teeth and to implant artificial "fore-teeth," a skill he advertised in the *Boston Gazette.* He said he had fixed a hundred teeth and that his implants held up for eating (and smiling). Among his patients was Joseph Warren, into whose mouth Revere implanted two ivory teeth. Dentistry was in relative infancy then, and a person who had options, as Warren did, chose a dentist based on trust and confidence in his skill. After Warren was fatally shot at Bunker Hill, British soldiers, who so despised Warren for his leadership of the rebels, for what they considered his seditious views, bayoneted him beyond recognition in his grave. It was by the dental work, those ivory teeth he had implanted some seven years before, that Revere would identify Warren's body.

Jonathan Singleton Copley's Paul Revere

4

PORTRAIT OF THE ARTISAN AS A YOUNG IRREVERENT

There are numerous depictions—sketches, drawings, paintings, sculptures—of an imagined Paul Revere riding horseback through the villages and farms of Middlesex. And there is one contemporary portrait of Revere as a young man. Oil on canvas, it was painted by John Singleton Copley over multiple sittings during the charged, uncertain year of 1768 in Boston. It's a rich rendering. Revere's seated and slightly angled, his face half-cast in shadow. Right eyebrow possibly cocked, right hand up at the chin, elbow on the table before him. The folds and gatherings of his white work shirt are expertly drawn. His waistcoat's unbuttoned. He's cradling a silver teapot in his left hand, burins on the table before him. The portrait gives a sense of depth and warmth, and of a person caught just so, that is consistent with the best of Copley's work. The canvas is about three feet tall, just under two and a half feet wide, and it hangs prominently in the Museum of Fine Arts in Boston, which received the painting from Revere's descendants and has held it in its collection for close to one hundred years.

Copley was the preeminent portrait artist of colonial America, his work coveted and most often commissioned by, or for, men and women of significant wealth or of political or religious standing. Revere's portrait hangs in the museum near Copley's portrayals of John Hancock, Samuel Adams, and Joseph Warren. Copley finished more than 125 portraits during his years in America before the Revolution. A representative sampling of his subjects might include the prominent landowner Moses Gill, the heiress Mary Sherburne, the well-married goods trader Nathaniel Sparhawk, the politician Martin Howard, and, also in 1768, the high-born commander in chief of the British army in America, Thomas Gage. Copley is known to have painted five subjects that year: Gage, the wealthy merchants John Amory and George Watson, the loyalist Anglican priest Myles Cooper, and Revere.

Revere is the one who is not like the others. Among

those 125 Copley portraits only 15 depict artisans or skilled tradesmen. Most of those fifteen portraits Copley produced earlier than 1768, before he was fully established as an artist. To have one's portrait painted by Copley in the late 1760s was expensive, much more expensive than Revere could have afforded. In 1768 he documented just £40 in earnings from his work as a silversmith, engraver, and dentist—a modest income for a married man with five children, and the lowest yearly income Revere recorded during that time. By way of comparison, in 1762 he had earned more than seven times that amount, specifically £294.

Lowered income and financial uncertainty marked the economy that year in Boston, reeling as it was in the aftermath of the 1767 Townshend Acts, which taxed, among other items, paint, paper, and tea. (It's no accident that Copley depicts Revere with a teapot.) The same year he sat for Copley's portrait Revere shaped and engraved the Liberty Bowl on commission by the Sons of Liberty (the fervent colonists' rights and antitax organization to which Revere belonged) and in homage to the Massachusetts Assembly for its rejection of the Townshend Acts. It's possible, even likely, that Revere paid for Copley's portrait through bartering. His ledger shows various silversmith work done for Copley (plates, spoons, chalices) around this time.

That Revere would even seek to have such a portrait

made may have been as a way to further advertise his silversmith work to the Boston elite—the stubbornly moneyed class who traditionally turned to London for items of silver and gold, but who now, either to join the boycott of British goods that the Townshend Acts engendered among the colonists, or simply to be served more quickly, would have sought a high-quality local alternative. Revere looked the right sort in the portrait. And the gleaming silver teapot, its spout and finial exquisitely etched, conveyed, along with its political allusion, a touch of luxury. The portrait, done as it was by the city's leading artist, indicated that as a silversmith Revere could meet a wealthy man's demands.

BECAUSE IT IS the only portrait of a young Revere, our only potentially accurate glimpse of him to populate our collective imagination, it has received a fair amount of comment—regarding its setting, its style, and its suggestion. "Seated behind a worktable, with engraver's tools before him, Revere is at once maker and thinker," writes Jane Kamensky in *A Revolution in Color: The World of John Singleton Copley*. "Highly finished and elaborately staged, the portrait is a paradox, dazzling in its seeming modesty." Some posit that Revere's direct look toward the viewer represents his engagement with a customer at his shop at Clark's Wharf. Others suggest he's gazing more ruminatively, out toward Boston through the window seen reflected in the upper curve of the teapot.

What's notable about the portrait here, why it is relevant to understanding the man who would risk all that he had when he mounted a horse on the opposite shore that mid-spring night of 1775, is what it shows—what it declares—about Revere's attitude toward class. Bring the portrait to your mind's eye and you might swear he is winking at you, although he isn't. Unless he is. The hint of a raised eyebrow, the points of light in his eyes, the suggestion of a smile suppressed. Copley was that fine and purposeful a painter. Revere is dressed and positioned in a way that at once alludes to a hands-on artisan in his milieu, yet might also project a dilettante. There's not a stain or smudge on Revere's clothes. His fingers appear smooth and unmarked. His hands and wrists look soft. He's not in the right worker's outfit. He's foppish, even. A gentleman in satire.

For Revere the value that society placed on class, on high breeding as it were, was a value to be lampooned. The class strata of colonial Boston, a pulsing carryover from British society, thrived even as the principles of the Revolution, and the principles of those in the trenches of the Revolution, would have done away with such strata altogether. Revere came from neither British pedigree nor forefather stock. Neither did Copley; his single mother ran a tobacco shop. Both were self-made men.

Long before he sat for Copley's portrait, Revere took it upon himself to refashion his family crest. Apollos Rivoire had created, as his signature bookplate, an engraving of a French coat of arms. To this Revere added a British Barbary lion, not roaring but laughing. He added the Gallic cock, alighting frivolously, its wings a-flapping. And he added a loosely connected military mantra, *Pugna pro Patria,* "I fight for the fatherland," which was then aligned most prominently with the Dutch. Sure, he'd fight for the fatherland! But which fatherland exactly? Revere would have a family crest, all right, but not one to be taken too seriously.

Years later when describing certain pre-Revolutionary activities that he and fellow artisans engaged in, Revere referred to himself and his peers as "mechanics," rather than the more common, and by then much more accurate, "artisan." *Mechanic,* meaning a person who did manual labor, was still a known term then. But it was a coarser term, less in use, and its implication did not suggest a skilled artisan. *Mechanic* in the late 1700s carried with it the distinct flavor of its earlier usage in England and the colonies, implying a low or even vulgar person. Revere chose the word in self-deprecation—*we were but lowly laborers*—thumbing his nose at the highfalutin.

It was by dint of his skill and unfailing work ethic, his confident, unpretentious nature, his loyalty, his smarts, and in high measure his passion and ingenuity for the rebellion that Revere would come to mix with John Hancock and Samuel Adams, to form a friendship with Joseph Warren. Revere supported their plans and aided their aims. He did their bidding, often for a fee. But Revere was never one of them, never on equal footing. Over the years Revere prospered, socially and financially, in the egalitarian network of caucuses and clubs, of like-minded men (and women) seeding the Revolution in Boston. And he prospered in a satisfying way, by gaining access to and respect from the elite, while never having to suffer the indignity of being so privileged himself. Revere was not born into land or money. He received no high-shelf education. He spent less time pondering. He worked. He could make a cup or a fork or a plate. He could fix your tooth. He could ride a horse.

No aspect of Copley's portrait proves more telling than Revere's right hand, its thumb and forefinger on either side of the chin. He sits as if in contemplation, as if in uffish thought. Rarely in his portraiture did Copley present a subject's hand in such a prominent point of focus. And rarely in the recent centuries of humankind has a sitting subject struck such a chin-stroking pose without irony. It's borderline unfathomable that Revere would have held this gesture in earnest. It's easy to imagine him doing it in jest.

Revere survives in that Copley portrait, in that winking pose, as he looked at age thirty-three, in the thick of his life in business and in resistance. A man among men. Still seven years from immortality. You step away from the portrait and you come back to it, and you recognize something of the irreverent. You get the strong feeling that Paul Revere is up to something.

"The Boston Massacre," engraved by Paul Revere

5

A CERTAIN RESOLVE

WHEN HE RODE, HE RODE ON HORSES RENTED OR borrowed, and he rode with specific intent, an assignment at hand. These were long rides. Well more than 225 miles to bring news from Boston to New York. Close to 350 miles from Boston to Philadelphia. And then back again. Revere learned to ride well and efficiently. He formed an understanding of when best to rest and water a horse and also, on those long journeys, an understanding of when best to change his mount. There's reason to suspect that Revere rode for recreation on open land outside Boston. At some point he bought for himself a middle-aged mare. He had to have practiced to get as good as he was on the back of a horse.

He rode at the bidding of the leaders of the Revolution, a foot soldier in the fertile fields of rebellion. Within Boston's Committee of Correspondence, the Patriot communication network driven into action by Samuel Adams, Revere was a beating heart. The committee's express riders spread messages on horseback throughout the towns and villages: a call to meeting for local leaders, the notice of a larger gathering, an assessment—from Boston or Salem perhaps—of redcoat activity, or news of some resolution or action on the part of the colonists.

In the immediate aftermath of the Boston Tea Party, mid-December of 1773, Revere rode from Boston to New York, then on to Philadelphia, to bring the details of what the Patriots had done and what they wanted it to mean. He was a durable rider, sat easy in the saddle, and he covered ground as well as any other man on the committee. Revere brought with him not only the momentous report from Boston Harbor but also a talent for describing it. "Paul Revere will give you all the news," John Adams once said. Revere spoke directly and essentially, without embellishment yet with the brio of a believer. He was congenial enough in manner but did not gabble and did not delay. Eleven days after he'd set off to the south that December, Revere arrived back in Boston, seven hundred miles of travel behind him and bearing the critical, full-throated approval of Patriot peers.

"Mr. Paul Revere returned from New York and Philadelphia, performing his journey in much shorter time than could be expected at this Season of the year," wrote the Boston diarist John Boyle. "The inhabitants of these Cities were highly pleased with the Conduct of the People here in destroying the Tea and they were determined that when the Tea Ships expected there arrive, they should be Immediately returned to the Place from whence they came."

The Boston Tea Party, which Revere took part in, and the news of it, which Revere brought south, proved to be the event that more than any other accelerated the unification of the factious American colonies, that brought them closer to one for the fight against the British. Revere billed the Committee of Correspondence 4 pounds, 10 shillings, for his expenses on the round trip to Philadelphia, and 4 pounds, 16 shillings, for the hiring of the horses, and another 4 pounds, 16 shillings, as payment for his time. He needed every pence of it, though he could easily have charged more. The total fee of 14 pounds, two shillings, was quickly and gratefully approved, underwritten for the committee by John Hancock, the wealthiest Boston Patriot of all.

* * *

REVERE'S WIFE, SARAH, had died in May of 1773, and then their last child together, a baby girl they'd named Isannah, died in late summer. In October, Revere married Rachel Walker. She was twenty-seven and Revere was thirty-eight, and they would remain together for forty years, for the rest of her life. Revere wrote Rachel adoring poems and dropped endearments into his letters home. She might sign hers to him "adieu, my love." It was Rachel, along with Revere's mother, who was at their home in the North End caring for Sarah's six surviving children and pregnant with the first of her own when, in mid-May of 1774, five months past the Tea Party, Revere traveled that long route—Boston to New York to Philadelphia, and back up to Boston—once again.

He changed his mount at King's Bridge, the northern edge of New York, and later crossed by ferry the river from New York to New Jersey. On this journey he went to tell of the arrival at Boston Harbor of the twenty-gun British ship *Lively* and how the *Lively*'s presence augured the imminent closing of the Boston port. The port was being shut down by Britain as punishment, until the colonists paid for the ninety-two thousand pounds of tea they had destroyed—a payment the colonists had no intention to make. Without an open, active port, little livelihood was to be had around Boston. "The people receive this cruel edict with abhorrence and indignation," wrote Samuel Adams to James Warren, who was part of the Committee of Correspondence. "I hope they will sustain the blow with a becoming fortitude, and that the cursed design of intimidating and subduing the spirits of all America, will, by the joint efforts of all, be frustrated." In other words, *It's time to take a stand.*

The British imposed other measures that spring and summer. The Coercive Acts all but dissolved the Massachusetts charter, concentrated power in the hands of loyalist judges and politicians, granted greater strength and purview to the Crown-appointed Massachusetts governor, Thomas Gage, and forbade the colonists from holding town meetings. The British shut down Boston's waterways—no boat in or out, no parcel of food or materials could so much as cross the Charles River. In June, the Quartering Act decreed that British soldiers could take over public buildings or private barns as places to live. It applied not only to Massachusetts but to all of the colonies, and it established in the most conspicuous manner the presence of military rule.

With each decree and imposition, the American animosity toward the Crown intensified, and those who were ready to join in rebellion grew in number. Towns from Canada to the southern colonies sent gifts to Boston that the people there might hold firm: barrels of rice from South Carolina, bushels of wheat from Quebec, flour from Virginia, cattle and sheep from outlying New England towns. Boston. Providence. Newport. Hartford.

New York. Baltimore. Philadelphia. Charleston. A coalescence had begun.

It was in that spirit, to strengthen even more the bonds across the miles, that Revere rode south once again in the summer of 1774, though this time only as far as New York. There, he stayed, as he had before, with John Lamb, a fellow engraver, a fellow member of the Sons of Liberty, and a partner on the Committee of Correspondence. Lamb had been rallying against British imperialism for years. He knew how to organize and rouse a faction of men. In New York, Revere also met with Isaac Sears, another ardent leader of the Sons of Liberty, and another man who could mobilize a mob.

The power of Revere's visit came not from the passing of specific news but rather from the conference with Lamb and Sears and others—the acknowledgment of the population's widening discontent, and the further aligning of the paths to resistance. Revere made this trip in a manner uncommon for him: traveling by sulky, thus sparing his body the chafing of another days-long ride. A soft chair was the seat of a sulky and looser were the reins. Revere could steer his horse through creek and marsh along the Post Road, stop the sulky and scotch the wheels, and take his lunch in the tree shade or by an off-road swale to escape the summer sun.

As carriages went, the sulky proved light and built for speed. Revere could travel with purpose—he was gone from Boston less than twelve days on that summer journey—though not of course with the speed of traveling on horseback. A sulky journey aside, Revere invariably sat astride a Narragansett Pacer, the breed that most other express riders rode as well. The Narragansett was bred for endurance and agility. Despite a high step, awkward to the eye, the horse loped and galloped effectively over uneven terrain. "They pace naturally though in no very graceful or easy manner," wrote the statesman Edmund Burke. These were hardy horses, smaller than the working horses of today, swift when called upon, and not easily tired. For Revere's long journeys, and for other rides, too, the Narragansett Pacer was a horse he could depend upon.

Now it was September 11, 1774, and Revere was in the saddle once more, again southward bound, riding first to the town of Milton, ten miles from home, with the swiftness of the journey front of mind. Joseph Warren had called for him, and Revere knew why.

The nineteen towns of Suffolk County—the Massachusetts county that included Boston and Charlestown and from there dipped inland and southwest—had approved the Suffolk Resolves, a 2,061-word, twenty-paragraph declaration unlike any that had come before. The Resolves put a point on the American rejection of the acts and mandates that the Crown had lately imposed. The Resolves all but dismissed allegiance to Britain as a governing body. They came within a careful breath of declaring war.

From their opening words, the Resolves spoke without restraint. "Whereas the power but not the justice, the vengeance but not the wisdom of Great-Britain, which of old persecuted, scourged, and exiled our fugitive parents from their native shores, now pursues us, their guiltless children, with unrelenting severity." This was by way of preamble.

Over several weeks and through several conferences Joseph Warren had written the words. The county leaders had gathered first at Doty's Tavern in Stoughton and then convened in Dedham, and finally in Milton, where Warren read the Resolves aloud, standing in the doorway of a merchant's home, to the cheering of the Suffolk delegates.

"The late acts of the British parliament . . . are gross infractions of those rights to which we are justly entitled by the laws of nature, the British constitution, and the charter of the province," the Suffolk Resolves declared early on. The text urged a boycott of British goods as well as a "steady, manly, uniform, and persevering opposition," while at the same time disavowing any engagement in "routs, riots, or licentious attacks upon the properties of any person." Most presciently the document advised that "the inhabitants of those towns and districts, who are qualified, do use their utmost diligence to acquaint themselves with the art of war as soon as possible."

Now Revere was called upon to travel his familiar route and deliver the Resolves to Philadelphia, without undue pause in New York or anywhere else along the way, making haste to the First Continental Congress in hopes that the delegates of the colonies would read the words and understand the size of the message and agree.

The day opened fair and cool, and the sun rose at Revere's back as he rode his first leg to Milton, received there a copy of the Resolves, and then continued along the wooded road, narrow at times and rough, toward Attleboro and Providence and to an inn for his first night's rest. His children might have spent the day at household chores and playing near the water off the North End. Rachel was now six months into pregnancy.

Already the representatives of twelve colonies, all save Georgia, had arrived in Philadelphia for the Continental Congress, a mix of men who were seeking greater and renewed conciliation with Britain and others who were seeking a firmer break toward colonial independence. The four men representing Massachusetts Bay included Samuel Adams and John Adams, who had traveled to Philadelphia at a more leisurely pace, partly by coach and partly on horseback. The journey was rough on Sam Adams, not a seasoned rider, who progressed deliberately and along the way needed extra padding to protect his soft behind.

Sam was the older of the cousins, turning fifty-two in the early autumn of 1774. John was thirty-eight. Sam loomed as the Patriots' full-throated political influencer, John as the pointed, no less passionate attorney. The Adamses' larger social thoughts were well aligned, their methods of a piece. Their differences, those of style and temperament, showed most visibly from up close. When Sam and John went around together, some people called them—and they sometimes called themselves—the Brace of Adamses.

At the gathering in Philadelphia, the Adams cousins embodied the full spirit of rebellion and revolution, even as many of the others on hand did not. As the Congress began, the delegates' general feeling seemed pitched toward adopting a plan to codify the union between Great Britain and America. The plan was put forth by the politically active loyalist lawyer Joseph Galloway of Pennsylvania, and those who supported the Suffolk Resolves intended to combat that plan.

The principles of the Resolves had taken on greater urgency in the days just before the Continental Congress. On the early morning of September 1, 1774, General Gage sent 260 British troops from Boston to the northern end of Charlestown. They rowed through darkness on the Mystic River, then made a mile-long march at dawn, to reach the largest powder house in Massachusetts. Swiftly the redcoats seized and removed some 250 half barrels of gunpowder. A splinter group marched on to Cambridge and took a pair of cannons stored there. The mission proved efficient and smooth, with no skirmish, yet word began to spread that the British had fired on colonists, that blood had been shed and lives lost. That day and in the days that followed, hundreds, then thousands, then tens of thousands, of men came toward Boston from towns and regions near and far, bearing a hunting gun or a flintlock pistol, ready to meet the redcoats where they were. "All along were armed men rushing forward, some on foot, some on horseback," the writer the Reverend Ezra Stiles chronicled, describing towns north of Litchfield, Connecticut. "At every house women and children making cartridges, running bullets, making wallets, baking biscuits, crying and bemoaning and at the same time animating their husbands and sons to fight for liberties, though not knowing whether they should ever see him again. . . . They scarcely left half a dozen men in a town, unless old and decrepit."

Thousands of rebels were gathered at Cambridge Common, restive but restrained, and thousands more were closing in, when they learned the truth: that the British soldiers had never raised their guns during the seizing of the powder house in Charlestown. Nor had anyone been hurt. With this understanding and seeing that the redcoats were not now out on an offensive but sticking to their Boston encampments, the rebels stood down and returned home. Yet the ferocity of the Patriots' intent, and their immediate willingness to fight, had been made dramatically clear. And the larger message of what had happened, that the British were forcibly taking possession of provincial gunpowder and cannon, fortifying their stores while depleting those of the colonists, felt ominous.

A few days after that momentous event, the Powder Alarm as it would be known, and shortly before he would set off with the Suffolk Resolves for Philadelphia, Revere wrote to John Lamb in New York, touching on what happened and its aftermath: "The Spirit of Liberty never was higher than at present; the Troops have the horrors amazingly, by reason of some late movements of our friends in the Country the week past." By "the Troops," to be clear, Revere meant the British.

As Revere rode the many miles carrying the Resolves to Philadelphia that next week, a supplement to the *Massachusetts Gazette* published the Suffolk Resolves in their entirety, engaging the wider public. Warren and the town delegates also sent a copy of the Suffolk Resolves directly to General Gage.

GENERAL. GOVERNOR. COMMANDER in chief. Thomas Gage had lived for two decades in America, arriving from

England with his regiment in 1755 to serve in the territorial fight against France in the French and Indian War. Gage was thirty-seven years old then, the son of a viscount and a lieutenant colonel who had done battle in the Low Countries of Europe and then taken a long post in Ireland. In America, Gage fought first in the Ohio Territory as part of the bitter, failed Battle of the Monongahela. He and the British Regulars did combat side by side with local American troops, Colonel George Washington among them. They were beaten back by Canadian troops and Native American men from the Ottawa, Shawnee, and Mingo tribes, and Gage was wounded twice—in his stomach and then by a shot that grazed his brow. As he and Washington led their men in retreat, they passed hundreds of bodies fallen on the ground around them.

In the years that followed, Gage ascended to brigadier general and then to major general. He served as governor of Montreal for a time and then, in 1764, with the French and Indian War won and behind them, Gage was appointed by King George as commander in chief of the British army in America. Gage lived in New York, and he proved—by the lights of London and white colonial America—a talented administrator, carrying out the will of Parliament and the Crown, facilitating and coordinating the defense of a vast region, diplomatic rather than bullheaded in negotiations with Native American tribes.

Gage had a long face and a sturdy chin and a confidence about the eyes. John Singleton Copley's portrait depicts Gage standing with a good-humored, kind expression, while at the same moment pointing toward a background scene of the Royal Army marching on a colonial town. Friendly enough but firm, seems to be the message. Charles Lee, a lieutenant in the Royal Army who then became a general, second-in-command to General Washington, in the Continental Army, once wrote to Gage, "I respected your understanding, lik'd your manners and perfectly ador'd the qualities of your heart." Gage sent his children to attend the more refined schools in England, but he also bought large parcels of land in New York where, he imagined, his descendants might live. When in 1773 Gage prepared to return to England for a spell, Patriot leaders, including Washington, attended a gathering for his send-off.

Tensions and tempers rose in Massachusetts Bay while Gage was away, and the specter of conflict appeared in full. In 1774, King George sent Gage back to America to take over as the military governor of Massachusetts Bay. Gage was to continue to lead the Royal Army and to enforce the Coercive Acts (known to outraged rebel Americans as the Intolerable Acts), the measures that led to the Suffolk Resolves. The hope was that Gage, still well-liked by both sides, might impose some discipline, some collective order, and find a way to assuage the champing colonists.

Gage saw to it that the Boston port was closed on time, that the redcoats were increasingly quartered throughout the city, that the colonial judicial system now tilted toward those appointed by the Crown. He added troops to the roads leading in and out of Boston. He ordered gunpowder and cannons to be seized into British control. Yet Gage aimed to govern with benevolence and understanding toward the Patriots. He held off from arresting the leaders of the radical movement. He censured his own soldiers when they grew unruly. He was known for having empathy for the other side. *Too soft,* some of the redcoats said, calling him in private Granny Gage.

YEARS EARLIER, IN 1758, while stationed south of New York, Gage had married an American-born woman of noted beauty and self-possession: Margaret Kemble, whose father was a prominent landowner in New Jersey and whose mother moved within the highest society in New York. Margaret Kemble's maternal lineage traced back well more than a century in America, to the 1630s. Her great-grandfather had been mayor of New York City. During the foreboding stages of the early 1770s Margaret Kemble Gage said that she "hoped her husband would not be instrumental in sacrificing the lives of her countrymen." This was according to Thomas Hutchinson, who preceded Thomas Gage as governor of Massachusetts Bay.

While the context and circumstances in which she said this are not entirely clear, the fact that by "countrymen" she meant those Americans in opposition to British rule, and not the loyalists, is not in doubt.

As a younger man in England, Gage had had his heart broken by a woman of high standing to whom he was engaged. And now his affection for Margaret Kemble Gage was abundant and without reserve. He was forty when they married, and she was twenty-four. Some among the British leadership referred to Margaret Kemble Gage as the Duchess. Others observed that General Gage behaved submissively in her presence. She was proud, charming, and not a woman who shied from attention. In her 1771 John Singleton Copley portrait she wears a suggestive, bejeweled headdress. Slender strings of pearls rest against her pale, plunging neckline. Her dark eyes look off toward somewhere else. Lovely, demure. The style of dress echoed a style seen at masquerade balls in Europe. And when the portrait of Margaret Kemble Gage traveled to England to be displayed, the portrait caused a stir.

All of this—the competing sentiments and perhaps underlying remorse that Thomas Gage felt for levying punishments against the colonists, and his special devotion to his strong-willed wife, and his wife's own competing feelings as well as her allegiance to American life—is of material interest to the ride of Paul Revere.

It is not known how the leaders of the Revolution, specifically John Adams, Samuel Adams, John Hancock, and Joseph Warren, became aware of when and to where Royal troops would be dispatched in April of 1775. None of the British soldiers and military commanders knew until the operation was nearly begun. Most didn't know until it was underway. When on the eve of the operation General Gage told Brigadier General Hugh Percy details of the plan, Gage said to Percy that he, Gage, had informed only one other person. Gage did not specify whom, but that person may have been Margaret Kemble Gage, to whom Gage was closer than anyone else. She understood the nuanced emotions he had about organizing the troops toward Lexington and Concord, knowing as he did what the operation might cause and to what it might then lead.

Margaret Kemble Gage would have been the most natural confidant to General Gage. And Margaret Kemble Gage may also have been the woman who—some days before the night of April 18, 1775—passed along the information that put the Minutemen and the local militia on general alert.

"A daughter of liberty, unequally yoked in point of politics, sent word, by a trusty hand, to Mr. Samuel Adams, residing in company with Mr. [John] Hancock at Lexington, about thirteen miles from Charlestown that the troops were coming out in a few days," wrote the Reverend William Gordon in his contemporary chronicling of the events. Gordon was a known pastor in Roxbury, and in 1775 he became chaplain to the Provincial Congress. He was close to (and closely aligned with) Samuel Adams and other colonial leaders. There may have been no other woman of that time and place, no other "daughter of liberty," at once so near to the corridors of power and so "unequally yoked in point of politics" as Margaret Kemble Gage. She feared the outcome of her husband's military intent, and she had the wealth and mechanism to have a message delivered to Samuel Adams.

There's no questioning her ambivalence. And within Margaret Kemble Gage's prominent family churned varying perspectives and levels of commitment. A cousin to Margaret Kemble Gage, Philip Schuyler, was entrenched on the rebel side, an active member of the Provincial Assembly, pursuing the self-governance of the colonies. Margaret Kemble Gage's father, while a loyalist, had personal connections to any number of Patriots and was so respected by the Continental Army that, despite his wealth and assets, they never badgered him as the war progressed and never seized his land.

Later in 1775, in the aftermath of the Battle of Bunker Hill—a battle won by the British at great loss of life—Margaret Kemble Gage suggested that she felt torn in much the same way that Blanche of Spain felt torn in

Shakespeare's *The Life and Death of King John*. Specifically, Margaret Kemble Gage recalled Blanche's words when considering imminent war between French and British forces:

The sun's o'ercast with blood. Fair day, adieu.
Which is the side that I must go withal?
I am with both, each army hath a hand,
And in their rage, I having hold of both,
They whirl asunder and dismember me.
Husband, I cannot pray that thou mayst win.—
Uncle, I needs must pray that thou mayst lose.—
Father, I may not wish the fortune thine.—
Grandam, I will not wish thy wishes thrive.
Whoever wins, on that side shall I lose.
Assurèd loss before the match be played.

Unequally yoked. Doubly yoked. Yoked in the most agonizing way.

Others have been suspected as the first leak to the British Regulars' movement that night. The Revolutionary War historian and author J. L. Bell, for example, makes a case in his excellent 1775 blog that an informant to Joseph Warren may have been William Jasper, a British-born cutlery merchant in Boston. The sun has set on determining with certainty who among the loyalists was the first to let the information out. Suspicion followed Margaret

Kemble Gage during the rest of her life, although some of her peers dismissed that suspicion entirely.

After nearly nine years without childbearing, Margaret Kemble Gage and Thomas Gage conceived two children together in the aftermath of April 18, 1775, the seventh and eighth children of their union. There's no plain indication of what might have rekindled their parental desires at this time, nor whether conceiving more children might have been a way to reaffirm their love after a trying experience. Back in England in the late 1770s, the Gages would remain married and living together until Thomas's death in 1787.

To imagine that Margaret Kemble Gage may have divulged information to Samuel Adams about the British designs on Lexington and Concord is not to imagine that she had long-term plans to betray her husband, nor that she had larger intent to undermine the British operation. It's not to imagine her in a life as a traitor or spy. What's quite possible to imagine is that as the prospect of real bloodshed neared, Margaret Kemble Gage experienced feelings of uncertainty and conflict, of dual loyalties much like Blanche of Spain, and that these feelings allowed her a momentary lapse at a time before the war began. It was a time when one could imagine that getting the right word to a Patriot leader might help to prevent the worst of it.

In August of 1775, four months after the colonial militias had routed the British out of Concord, and three months after they had inflicted such pain at the Battle of Bunker Hill, and with Boston under siege and the colonies in open rebellion—with the war, that is, in awful flower—Margaret Kemble Gage was sent by ship away from Boston and to live in England. General Thomas Gage, though, remained in America to command the Royal Army and try to win the war.

On the second day of his long ride to the First Continental Congress in Philadelphia, a day as equally warm and fair as the first, Revere continued south of Providence, into Connecticut, passing near the shoreline at times, and then back inland when the road broke that way. The route was often uneven and sometimes narrow, and the shaded areas along the sides of the roads were in some places still sodden from summer rains. Taverns appeared like landmarks and respites along the way. Norwich, Mohegan, New London, New Haven. At times Revere might have forded a stream or gully, through water chest-high on the horse, cooling them both. At the rivers near Groton and Waterford a rope ferry could have carried them across.

The weather broke on the third day of Revere's ride to Philadelphia, rain showers and a hard headwind. And the fourth day rose cooler still, a touch of frost upon the early-morning ground. Again, Revere changed his mount at King's Bridge, 234 miles from home. From the tavern there you could see pale green hills rising and falling and you could hear the rush of the river nearby. The rough roads lay better now around New York and better still as Revere rode on toward Philadelphia, now in his fifth day of traveling, a Friday. The day was sunny and fine once more as Revere covered the last miles on his fresh horse, passing along the banks of the Delaware where black walnut trees grew in crooked rows, then crossing that river, and arriving, dirty and dusty and tired, with the Suffolk Resolves in hand, to Arch Street, at the center of the city, where John Adams and Samuel Adams were lodged. "Mr. Revere brought us the spirited and patriotick resolves of your county of Suffolk," Samuel Adams wrote to pastor Charles Chauncy in Boston. "We laid them before Congress."

At the reading of the Resolves, "I saw tears gush into the eyes of the old, grave Pacific Quakers of Pennsylvania," wrote John Adams in his diary. Others there took a step back or inhaled. A frisson ran through the Congress—chilling some, enervating others—as the delegates grasped what the words might mean and what they all had in front of them.

And what went through the heart of General Thomas Gage at the moment that *he* read the Suffolk Resolves? Did he already know then? Could he see his fate? Could he see Great Britain's? Did Gage already know that the larger fight would one day be lost? Had he known that since the day barely a week before when he saw all the men, the farmers and carpenters and wheelwrights and pastors, who had assembled in arms and girded themselves in response to the Powder Alarm? Every man in the countryside it seemed—all but the "old and decrepit"—had quickly mobilized and were ready to fight and to die for the cause. Or did the Suffolk Resolves first deliver to Gage the grim epiphany? In that document of rebellion he could see all the strength of conviction, the disdain and bottled anger, the depth and detail, of the Patriot leaders' thought.

Thomas Gage knew—knowing in the way that a ship's captain knows when he recognizes an irreparable break in the hull that the ship's fate is sealed. The British imperialists were already done for. These new willful Americans, driven by their sense of righteousness and indignation, were going to rout their motherland, however long it might take.

"Civil government is near its end. . . . Conciliating, moderating, reasoning is over. Nothing can be done but by forceable measure," Gage wrote that week in a letter to London. He ordered "all available" Royal troops to come up to Boston from New York. He ordered two regiments of men to sail down from Quebec. Earlier in 1774, while on his sabbatical in England, Gage had brashly told

King George that he could contain the Patriots with little more than two thousand men. But now, in the wake of the Suffolk Resolves, he wrote to the British secretary of war, "If you think ten thousand men sufficient, send twenty. If one million is thought enough, give two. You will see both blood and treasure in the end." For Gage a cold cast of desperation was already setting in.

After the Continental Congress endorsed the Suffolk Resolves, Revere rode with that news back to Boston, carrying also letters from John Adams and Samuel Adams and the other Massachusetts Bay delegates. "Passed unanimously," Samuel Adams wrote, for publication in the *Boston Gazette.*

Revere would ride to Philadelphia once more that fall, again to the Continental Congress. He returned to Boston in late October with more news of the proceedings and with a thundering letter from Samuel Adams to Gage underscoring once more that when the Patriots described Great Britain's Coercive Acts as Intolerable, they meant it literally. Wrote Adams to Gage, "These Enormities, committed by a standing army, in our opinion, unlawfully posted there in a time of Peace, are irritating in the greatest Degree, and if not remedied, will endanger the involving all America in the Horrors of a civil War!"

As its final act the Continental Congress ratified and sent a petition to King George III, rebuking and seeking freedom from all aspects of the Coercive Acts, and other laws that unfairly burdened their lives. The Patriots vowed once more a boycott of British goods if the situation was not improved. Yet even then the delegates pledged a fragile, fading fealty to the Crown: "Your royal authority over us and our connection with Great Britain we shall always carefully and zealously endeavor to support and maintain."

On October 26, 1774, with that missive sent, the First Continental Congress closed its session. This was five months and twenty-three days before the night of April 18, 1775. In terms of the mood and stakes of the conflict—the Crown's bullying insistence, the Patriots' disposition and defiance—the stage was set.

The HMS Somerset *on the Charles River*

6

THE SOMERSET

LIFE BEGAN FOR HMS *SOMERSET* ON THE EASTern bank of the Medway River, her keel laid in the spring of 1746 at the Royal Dockyard in Chatham, twelve nautical miles from the mouth of the open sea. The great ship would be built from the wood of two thousand trees, elm for the massive keel, oak for the rest of her. The *Somerset* classed as a sixty-eight-gun warship, third rate, her seasoned timbers fastened by treenails that ran as long as three feet, and were as thick as two inches in diameter. She was launched by designation in the summer of 1748 and embarked on her maiden voyage from the harbor at Plymouth on a Saturday, April 26, 1755—or, to put the proper point on it, nineteen years, eleven months, and twenty-three days before the night of April 18, 1775, when the *Somerset* would loom, swinging wide at her moorings, her masts and spars outlined against the moon, in the narrow channel between Boston and Charlestown. She had her duty guard assigned that night, forecastle to quarterdeck, to watch for any provincial who might attempt to cross the channel and escape the locked-down city. That of course is what Paul Revere would try to do, stealthily in the moonlight, fixing to reach the opposite shore and begin the ride of his life.

Full rigged and 160 feet in length, the *Somerset* carried more than two dozen thirty-two-pound cannons, just as many eighteen-pounders, a dozen nine-pounders, and some four-pound swivels. From the upper gun deck a skilled gun captain on a third-rate ship could crush a target from a quarter mile out. The crew, four hundred men or more when a mission began, were armed with pistols, muskets, and blunderbusses and enough powder in the hold to fight for days. Four hundred crewmen, but enough room, if needed, for twice that many. In 1757, three years into the French and Indian War, the *Somerset* overwhelmed a French warship bound for Quebec and brought 360 prisoners on board.

The *Somerset* fought gallantly all through the French

and Indian War. She got the better of many enemy vessels. She took a merchant ship off the tip of Newfoundland. She battered back French privateers—first the *Dauphiness,* then the *Victorie*—that were headed for Cape Breton Island. At the Siege of Louisbourg in 1758, the event that historians say broke the French and turned the war irrevocably to the British, seamen from the *Somerset* helped seize the last French warships in the theater, burning the *Prudent* as it lay aground at Louisbourg harbor, and helping to tow off the defeated *Bienfaisant* under British command. The following year, 1759, the Somerset sailed as part of the British fleet that captured Quebec.

And in the last years of the war until the Treaty of Paris was signed in 1763, the *Somerset,* having seen so much confrontation in the Atlantic, was assigned to patrol the Strait of Gibraltar, a quieter arena, where under the warmth of the North African sun she intercepted smaller, often lightly armed ships that were bound for France, carrying supplies.

HMS *Somerset,* which could bear close to fifteen hundred tons in calm waters, proved hardy and resolute despite a long run of sustained damage and some misfortune. At Plymouth harbor, before the maiden voyage to Canada in 1755, the *Somerset*'s longboat was pierced in three places during a routine lowering, an accident that wounded several crewmen. A book about the *Somerset,* written by Marjorie Hubbell Gibson and drawing from contemporary logs and repair records, reports how on the return from that voyage—a monthlong autumn sail from Halifax to southern England—thunderous waves pounded the *Somerset*'s decks, washing overboard chests of arms, cannonballs, and bags of shot. The longboat needed to be heaved off to lighten the ship's load. Windowpanes were shattered, the mainsail split, the compass binnacle snapped. This was just the first of the squalls. Time and again over the years the *Somerset,* much like other warships that crossed the Atlantic through the treacherous fall and winter months, was buffeted by raging storms and unrelenting gales. Time and again she was taken in to shore to be caulked and repaired, refurbished, and retrimmed.

Men suffered and died on the *Somerset,* as they did on all warships. Some were tossed into the sea by the roiling waves or were cut by a fallen spar. Others became wasted by scurvy or smallpox or venereal disease, or other sicknesses they had no name for. Working in icy winds, the seamen suffered from chilblains and fever and sores.

Some men simply leaped over the side and into the briny deep, better to end things than to endure the barbs and trials of that daily life. Rules were strict and justice uneven. Seamen were flogged for trespasses small and large—thievery, drunkenness, negligence, sodomy. A crewman suspected of treason or desertion might be tied to a mast and lashed for all to see.

In the years following the French and Indian War the

Somerset was dry-docked, brought into the yard to undergo the most extensive of her repairs. Her immense hull was resealed, her rigging fully remade. Gibson reports that the work wasn't complete for nearly eight years, a period of healing for the *Somerset* as it were, of convalescence. In the early 1770s, rehabbed and seaworthy, the *Somerset* was deployed as a guardship in an estuary of England's Tamar River. That's where she was, at relative rest, in December 1773 when across the Atlantic Patriot rebels tossed the tea into Boston Harbor, and the provincials in Massachusetts Bay began to organize in greater earnest, newly determined and powerful. The unrest in the colonies was now registering ever more seriously and ominously in the minds of the Crown. Greater conflict felt imminent, and something had to be done.

And so it was that on October 19, 1774, with the Suffolk Resolves having been embraced by the Congress in Philadelphia and General Thomas Gage clamoring for support, the *Somerset* was put to sail in the open ocean, a man-of-war.

The life and experience that the *Somerset* had hosted and absorbed over the decades could be seen on her timbers and markings. Old wood lay dark against the new. Thin, deep scars ran across the surfaces of the ship. Her sealed hull held sturdy and strong but was not, as the seamen would learn, impervious. She had new topsails, hoisted by new ropes, and she had a crew now of more than five hundred men, among them a detachment of marines. So primed, the *Somerset,* alongside the *Asia* and the *Boyne,* two other third-rate warships of His Majesty's fleet, crossed the Atlantic once again, and once again through high winter winds. This time, however, she was bound for Boston.

SHE SAILED FOR two full months, encountering immediate gales, losing the *Boyne,* then finding her again, taking on water, suffering a split in her topsail and a broken block at her foresheet. A seaman went overboard, a marine was lashed for theft. She came into sight of land—the northern reach of Cape Cod—through snowfall and hail, the crew bailing water when leaks could not be plugged, until, finally, on the suddenly clear and moonlit night of December 19, 1774, the *Somerset* came safely aground at Boston's Castle Island. She rested overnight, and the next day, bright but cold, she came to anchor in Boston Harbor, alongside other ships in the fleet—the *Asia* and the *Boyne,* the *Preston,* the *Glasgow,* the *Lively.* "The Yankys were exceedingly disappointed at seeing the *Somerset,* as they were in hopes she was lost," wrote the British lieutenant John Barker in his diary, adding, "The Harbour now cuts a formidable figure, having four Sail of the Line, besides frigates and sloops and a great number of transports."

British ships had floated menacingly in Boston Harbor for years, ever since they'd arrived in a flotilla over a couple of days in 1768. Revere's popular engraving of that landing-of-the-troops scene, a rendering he'd created from a drawing by the artist Christian Remick, showed the warships aligned in a crescent on the outer edge of the harbor, their hulls depicted in reddish wood, their flags out at bow and stern. Rowboats are shown bringing redcoats to shore, while smaller sloops and vessels bob alongside the docks, the city and its churches behind them. Revere first sold the engraving in April of 1770, in the aftermath of the Boston Massacre, and he inscribed the print with a cheeky, even sneering dedication, "To the Earl of Hillsborough, His Majests. Secy. Of State for America. This View of the only well Plan'd Expedition, formed for supporting ye dignity of Britain & chastising ye insolence of America, is hum'y Inscrib'd."

It was an exercise in satire, of mockery and seething. Revere added other language on the engraving describing the redcoats coming ashore, armed with guns and powder, in an "insolent parade."

And now at the dawn of 1775, Royal warships were again positioned just so in the harbor waters, six of them as well as the many smaller vessels. Other armed British ships sailed up and down the seaboard. The *Scarborough* and *Canceaux* were off the coast of New Hampshire. The *Rose* and the *Swan* in Rhode Island, the *Fowey* in Virginia.

The *Kingfisher* in New York. No warship was larger nor more heavily armed than HMS *Somerset.*

She remained moored in Boston Harbor all through the early months of 1775, as winter moved uneasily into spring. The men on board the ship "are in general very healthy," reported the British vice admiral Samuel Graves in a January dispatch to the House of Commons. The ship, however, remained less so. "The *Somerset* was so leaky at sea that two hand pumps were continually at work," Graves wrote, "and it is the constant employment at present of one hand pump to keep her free."

The *Somerset*'s crew operated under the command of Captain Edward LeCras. The marines answered to Major John Pitcairn, who was quartered in the North End, in a home directly next to the home of Paul Revere. In late February the *Somerset* held on board a court-martial in which LeCras and the captains of the surrounding ships acquitted a lieutenant charged with shooting to death a seaman who had tried to desert.

Snow and sleet still fell in early April when, to properly repair the *Somerset* for what missions lay ahead, two transport ships were brought up alongside her. The crewmen off-loaded all of the *Somerset*'s arms and all of her stores so that she could be lightened enough to heel. Carpenters arrived from other ships and trimmed her by the stern. They tore off the sheathing on the starboard side, around the leakage, and replaced rotted wood and caulked the *Somerset* until the leaks were finally stopped and she could be resheathed and righted. The crewmen loaded her guns and cannons back on board. And then a few days later, on April 15, 1775, the *Somerset,* now suitably fitted and honestly armed, was warped into the channel between the North End and Charlestown. She was moored there by cables to the land on either side, her yards and topmast installed, her shape great and threatening in the narrow waterway, a huge black hulk.

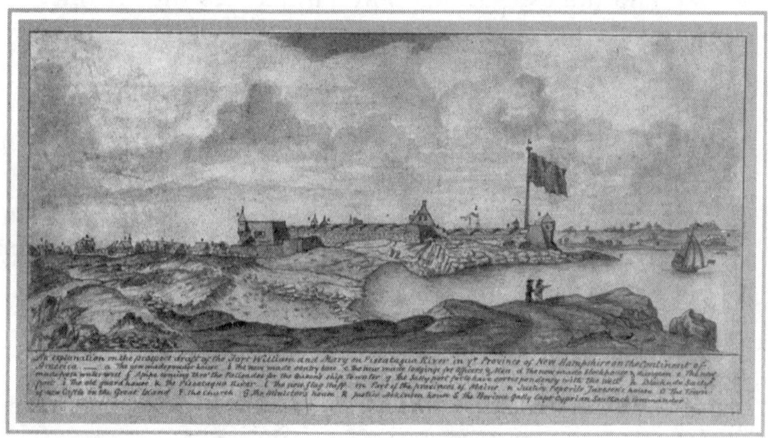

Fort William and Mary

7

PORTSMOUTH, DECEMBER 1774

WAS THIS WHERE THE AMERICAN REVOLUTION began, on a rocky outcropping against the cold, hard-rushing waters of the Piscataqua River on a blustering wintry afternoon? Was it here, alongside Portsmouth, New Hampshire, mid-December of 1774?

The colonists raised the level of their rebellion here, engineering their first organized act of aggression and direct defiance, drawing the first British shots. Hundreds of men in the Patriots' local militia moved in to take the ammunition, the powder, the small guns, and the cannon out of old Fort William and Mary. The fort, perched hard by the river's edge, was manned by only a handful of British guards. What greater protection was needed in times of peace? The guards put up a game but inevitably futile resistance as the rebels came over the walls and had their way on the grounds, took what they came for. This act, as New Hampshire's incensed Royal governor, John Wentworth, proclaimed, was "in open Hostility and direct Oppugnation [*sic*] of His Majesty's Government, and in the most atrocious Contempt of his Crown and Dignity."

The raiding of Fort William and Mary began on the bitter afternoon of December 14, 1774, and resumed one night later, through biting winds on the cusp of a New England winter. When it was over, the Patriots had a store of weapons that they would come to rely on in the months ahead, that they would deploy in mounting their resistance at Bunker Hill. And it happened, this successful and portentous raid, on the strength of a message delivered to Portsmouth by Paul Revere.

He rode north out of Boston on a gray afternoon, saddled on a gray horse, over hard and rutted land, riding with an urgency rare even for those urgent times. All through that year, the Royal Army had begun making its claim, girding and arming for the time ahead. Still fresh and caustic were the implications of the Powder Alarm,

General Gage's seizure of a store of gunpowder held outside Boston three months before. And now there was this: a directive from King George III, issued October 19, and just now come to light, that, first, forbade the importing of arms, gunpowder, or other "military stores" from Great Britain into the colonies, and, second, suggested that the Royal Army secure or seize any existing supplies of weapons already on American soil.

The king's letter was circulating among the Royal governors of the colonies and had been leaked to the Patriots. British warships were sailing toward Newport, Rhode Island, intent on taking over Fort George. The Patriots there had received back-channel word from Boston—"300 soldiers more or less are embarked for Newport"—and so had already begun to gather and hide Fort George's cache: three tons of lead, forty thousand flints, three hundred barrels of gunpowder, some fieldpieces. It was believed that other British ships were now sailing toward Fort William and Mary. For Revere, Boston to Portsmouth meant better than sixty miles of hard riding, and he had to get there quickly.

He had met with Samuel Adams and Joseph Warren to go over what they knew and had then left the men in colloquy at the Green Dragon and slipped off by ferry, out of the harbor and across the Mystic River, then mounted the gray horse and set out along the Salem Road. Revere had all the pressing information to deliver—specifically of King George's decree, and of the need for immediate Patriot action—and he carried in his saddlebag a letter written by Warren and signed in witness by William Cooper, the clerk of the town meeting. "The vigilance of our enemies is well known," Warren wrote. "If they can get our fortresses, our arms, and ammunition into their custody, they will despise all our attempts to shake off our fetters."

What was this now, the ninth ride Revere had taken on behalf of the rebel cause, the seventh in a little more than a year? Or was it ten altogether? Eleven? Revere wasn't counting—although in another sense he was. The missions weren't solely for the advancement of the movement and its principles. They also generated income. For his trip and stay in Portsmouth, and then a quick nip to Dorchester and Watertown later in the month, Revere would bill 5 pounds, 14 shillings. That covered the horse, his expenses, and about 2 pounds, 8 shillings for his time. Revere had seven children living under the roof of his North End house. Six of them, five girls and a boy, had been born to Sarah. (Two other girls had died in infancy.) And now, a little more than a year into their marriage, Paul and Rachel Revere had their first child together, a son, Joshua, born on December 7, 1774, five days before the start of this ride to Portsmouth. To net nearly two and a half pounds in a week as an express rider was not irrelevant. As an artisan in 1774, through his engraving, his smithing, and his dentistry, Revere earned 121 pounds.

The world around Revere, the circumstances, could feel precarious. And often ominous. British soldiers were now more among them than ever before, quartering in so many Boston homes. In the large brick house next door to the Reveres, Francis Shaw had been made to take in Major John Pitcairn, a commander of six hundred British marines. One of Pitcairn's officers, Lieutenant Wragg, had moved in as well. Shaw was a tailor by trade, wealthy, and he kept a family pew at the Old North Church. He was also a rebel, virulently anti-British in his heart.

Yet this was still a time when loyalists and colonists might gather in social spirit, and at Shaw's house gather they did. On any evening, Pitcairn and Revere might have found themselves side by side in the Shaws' front room. If Pitcairn proved to be a man of abiding good nature, sympathetic in his way, a churchgoer, and warm to the Shaws, he was no less resolute in his loyalty to the Crown. For Revere and his neighbor Francis Shaw, there was no softening the matter of Pitcairn's enforced presence as a British major in the Shaw home. With each encounter, however benign, was the knowledge of all that was at hand, and of why it was that Pitcairn and his marine command were there in Boston. Redcoats moved thickly all through the city then, North End, South End, West End, and East.

Since the middle of September, since he had ridden back from Philadelphia and the First Continental Congress's audacious passage of the Suffolk Resolves, Revere had joined with a few dozen men to form, as he described it, "a committee for the purpose of watching the movements of the British soldiers and gaining every intelligence of the movements of the Tories." So, there was reason beyond civility for a Patriot to raise a glass beside a British army major, or to amble alongside him out of church. Who knew what the British army major might let slip? During the nights of that autumn of 1774, members of the committee broke into pairs and patrolled the Boston streets, spies in the meager city light.

Revere was thirty-nine years old. He had the businesses and his children, and a second marriage rooted in love. Revere's mother lived with them as well. He served as the senior grand deacon of the Massachusetts Grand Masonic Lodge, a coveted position Revere had sought and aspired to and then kept through five elections over five years. For many men at other times and places in history—indeed for most men at most times and in most places—such a life, with a large family and with that purposeful social engagement and with work that conferred respect and success, might have made for a life more than full enough. But not now. This time and place demanded something more. Especially for a man as driven and intent and determined as Paul Revere.

* * *

He rode alone through the late afternoon and into the darkening night and would stop only in these hours to rest and water the horse. Past Salem, the road became the Boston Post Road, and this was now a way and a land that Paul Revere had not traveled before.

The December air warranted gloves for a rider, and woolen socks beneath the riding boots and an overcoat and hat. He rode by the favorable light of a gibbous moon and with stars clear enough to help him keep his bearings, and as he continued north and the night air grew colder, the ground became rougher still. At times great stands of trees, birch and pine, bracketed the road, and there were long, dark tenantless stretches, silent but for the hoofbeats and the jangling of the saddlebag and the whir of the wind. He rode past farmland and pastures bound by horse fences. A home or a barn set back from the road and outlined by the moonlight could give some shape and warmth to what a passing rider saw.

Revere could have made it to Amesbury that night, some forty miles north of Boston, and there fed and tied up the horse and lain down himself at the Amesbury Inn. Or he may have stopped sooner. The countryside was alive with Minutemen, and anyone would have known the name Paul Revere, and anyone would have given him a meal and a place to sleep. They knew of Paul Revere, express rider, in every town in Massachusetts Bay and the

Province of New Hampshire, and in every colony north of Virginia. They knew about Paul Revere—had seen his name in the papers—three thousand miles and an ocean away, in London, in Edinburgh, in Derbyshire.

On the next day, December 13, cold and overcast, Revere again rode the gray horse for many miles along the hardened Boston Post Road. Sleet fell, and snow, slowing their pace. Revere rode through Hampton and North Hampton and then came into Portsmouth, his horse spent and lathering from the effort. They rode onto the Portsmouth Parade, a promenade just inland from the line of docks that reached into the Piscataqua River. People walked about as evening approached, and Revere stopped and saw a man he recognized, William Torrey, who in the 1760s had been a shipbuilder in Boston. "He asked me in a hurry if I could inform him where he might find Samuel Cutts of Portsmouth, merchant," said Torrey a few weeks later when he was deposed and asked to give an account of this day. "Mr. Cutts happen[ed] to pass by at the time. I pointed to him, told Revere that was the man, upon which Revere set out after Cutts and presently overtook him. And to the best of my remembrance, they both went into Stoodley's Tavern together." Samuel Cutts belonged to a grand, long-standing Portsmouth family and was the head of the local Committee of Correspondence.

In Stoodley's Tavern, Revere took Warren's letter from his saddlebag and told Cutts all that he knew and what the committee in Boston believed. He showed Cutts a copy of the king's October 19 directive. Straightaway Cutts engaged others aligned with the cause, and a debate ensued about whether to go right then to Fort William and Mary, with as many men as they might gather in immediate haste, or rather to wait until the following day when more men could be assembled, and the mission might be better equipped and set. Little light was left in the sky and they couldn't be sure if the fort had already been reinforced by additional Royal soldiers. They decided to wait until the next day.

Revere left Stoodley's Tavern and returned to the Portsmouth Parade. Torrey was still there, waiting, and he asked Revere what the talk with Cutts had been all about. Torrey was a loyalist, and fiercely so. "He gave me for an answer that another man-of-war had arrived in Boston with a number of marines on board," said Torrey in his deposition. "And that it was conjectured by the inhabitants [of Boston] that they were bound for Piscataqua and had one or two men-of-war with them in order to take care of the powder and fort." Revere's implication was that the colonists meant to get control of the fort before any Royal warship arrived. Possibly Revere did not know that Torrey's sympathies lay with the Crown. Though as a rule when Revere was asked a question, by anyone, he answered honestly, bluntly, and in full.

It may be that Torrey—who would prove so hostile

to the rebel cause that in the next years, during the war, a sugar house he owned was vandalized and one of his ships was burned—went straight from the promenade to get word to Governor Wentworth of Revere's news.

By then, even aside from Samuel Cutts, some rebel leaders around Portsmouth may have learned of the king's intentions to take Fort William and Mary. The Marblehead Committee of Correspondence had also tried to send notice at about the same time that Revere left Boston. It was not a notice from Marblehead, however, that rallied the resistance. Revere did.

"Yesterday in the afternoon, Paul Revere arrived in this town, express from the committee in Boston," Governor Wentworth would write to General Gage in reporting the blistering siege upon Fort William and Mary. As Wentworth put it at the close of that letter, news of King George's mandate to seize the powder, and the call for the rebel militiamen to act in response, was all made public in Portsmouth "by the aforementioned Revere and the dispatch brought, before which all was perfectly quiet and peaceable here."

THE NEXT MORNING, December 14, the men were rallied together by drums beating on the Portsmouth Parade, a resounding call for soldier volunteers that brought them from all parts of Portsmouth, and then, as word spread, from Dover and Exeter and Rye. The rebels gathered noisily, arriving on horse and on foot, and laid plans to go to Fort William and Mary and forcibly take the stores. Arriving as well were prominent loyalists and government officials—the chief justice of the province, the secretary to Governor Wentworth—who warned the rebels in unwavering terms that they were conspiring to commit the highest act of treason. The Crown would hold them answerable for this treason for the rest of their lives. The rebels, scores of them now on hand, paid the warnings no mind. They carried muskets, pistols, and cutlasses.

The fort and its outer buildings occupied a little less than two acres and rose off the promontory at New Castle, an island parish of Portsmouth three miles from the heart of town. The men marched from the Portsmouth Parade to the docks and then pushed off for New Castle, rowing in scows and gundalows, broad-bottomed wooden boats with flat, open decks. The boats moved slowly on the rough waters of the Piscataqua, and as the rebels rowed, they were joined by other men on boats that had set out from other points and from the opposite bank at Kittery. The sky was dark for early afternoon, and on the approach the rebels could see, extending upward from the outcropping on the edge of the fort, an enormous British flag flapping heavily in the winter wind. In all, close to four hundred men landed at New Castle. They were led by thirty-three-year-old John Langdon, a

Portsmouth merchant who had lived at the mouth of the Piscataqua all his life and who had made his money in shipping.

Royal captain John Cochran had been posted at Fort William and Mary for three years, beginning the assignment long after the end of the French and Indian War, and up until this point he had never faced trouble of any kind. The night before, Governor Wentworth had sent notice to Captain Cochran of the potential siege by the rebels, and Cochran had quickly added two men to his usual command. Two men were all that he could find. There were now six loyalists in all to guard the fort, and before the rebels advanced, Cochran gathered those loyalists together. "I posted every man I had in the most advantageous station I could think of," Captain Cochran would later say under oath. "I ordered them not to flinch on pain of death but to defend the fort to the last extremity."

The fort's stone walls rose higher than six feet, up to eight feet at particular points. The fort was essentially rectangular, and in certain places the walls and embrasures were weathered and slightly crumbling, particularly on its eastern side, the side closest to the river. Chambers in the corners of the inner yard and in places where the fort was double-walled held the powder and the weapons, and there were areas for cooking as well as places to sleep. The yard itself was a flat lawn on which soldiers could assemble and stage during a conflict, and where Captain Cochran and his men took daily exercise during the long time of peace.

Vertical bars and a heavy wooden gate fortified the entrance on the inland side of the fort, and behind the gate stood a thick wooden door. Captain Cochran pointed four-pound cannons toward the entrance and pointed others outward through the embrasures in the direction from which he expected the militia to advance. The six Royal soldiers had loaded their muskets and fixed their bayonets.

A small group of rebels came first to the entrance of the fort, and John Langdon asked to be let in so that he might talk with Captain Cochran. Once inside, Langdon confirmed that the rebels intended to take the powder. When Cochran balked and asked to see an order from the king, Langdon—who would one day become the governor of New Hampshire—answered that he had "forgotten" to bring the order with him. Captain Cochran ordered Langdon to leave and threatened that if any among the herd of rebels "attempted to come into the fort their blood will be upon their hands, for I will fire on you." Langdon went out and the gate closed behind him.

For a moment, nothing happened at all. The local militia had surrounded the fort on all sides, and the British soldiers were at the ready and the gundalows were anchored in the low tide. The sky sat low, the color of slate, and gusts blew in off the river. It was three o'clock in the cold afternoon.

And then the signal was given—by Langdon it would seem—and the rebels started in on the fort, swarming over the walls in great numbers and dropping down onto the lawn. "The fort was stormed on all quarters . . . beset on all sides," Captain Cochran would say. His men fired the cannons, but none struck or injured anyone. They fired their muskets, also in vain, and then they were unable to reload before being engulfed. Rebels were everywhere, hundreds of them. One of Cochran's men, Isaac Seveay, got knocked down from the wall where he was stationed, disarmed, and confronted by a rebel with a pistol who told him to get on his knees and beg mercy. "When my legs are cut off below the knees and I cannot help it, but not before," Seveay responded.

Captain Cochran himself, a man of forty-four, held off capture for a time, brandishing his bayonet until he was taken and confined along with the others in the Royal command. The rebels were loud and invigorated and cheered as they pulled down the great British flag, colors that had flown from Fort William and Mary for more than one hundred years. They put out all the fires that warmed the barracks, and with axes and crowbars they tore down the door of the magazine where the barrels of gunpowder were stored. They found one hundred barrels and immediately began hauling them down to the water and loading them onto the gundalows. Each barrel weighed one hundred pounds. The rebels spent an hour and a half hauling and loading the barrels until the boats were fully laden, and then they began to push off and return upriver. Captain Cochran and his soldiers were set free, unharmed. It was suddenly quiet and dark at the fort with all the rebels gone and not a fire left burning.

THE NEXT DAY, as it eventually became known that no British reinforcements were imminent—two warships did sail up from Boston to New Castle, the twenty-gun HMS *Scarborough* and the eight-gun HMS *Canceaux*, but only days later—a second group of rebels advanced upon Fort William and Mary. This was a Thursday, December 15, and, it so happened, a day that in Massachusetts Bay had been designated a day of Public Thanksgiving. The designation did not come from the governor and the governing council as it had in previous years, but rather from the Provincial Congress and its leader, John Hancock. Many churches allied with or supportive of the Patriot leadership observed the Thanksgiving by holding special services. Preachers delivered sermons around themes of gratitude and humility. Closer to Portsmouth, in any number of New Hampshire towns, many men and women worked on their land and farms, salting beef, chopping wood, putting up a shed, carving a footpath through thicketed flats. The hard, varied work of near winter. The morning began cold and lowery, and in the afternoon a wet snow fell.

The rebels arrived at the fort around 10:00 P.M., having rowed their gundalows under the moonlight and with the tides. The night was again frigid, and windblown, but now the sky was clear. Although Captain Cochran tried to dissuade the rebels, suggesting deceitfully that the bulk of the fort's remaining stores consisted of old muskets that were of little or no use, the rebels instead found sixteen fine cannons along with cannon carriages and cannonballs, dozens of good muskets, some pistols, and other weapons of war. They spent all night and into the dawn loading the weapons onto the gundalows, until the tide was again in their favor and they rowed back upriver toward the town.

By now the gunpowder from the first day's siege was on its way to being loaded onto oxcarts and taken to where it could be kept and guarded. Over the following days it would be dispersed through the towns and villages of New Hampshire. Twenty-nine barrels would wind up in Exeter. Twelve barrels in Kingston, eight each in Epping and Nottingham, four in Portsmouth. Twenty-five barrels were hidden beneath the pulpit of the Durham meetinghouse. Londonderry got a few barrels. Brentwood. Poplin. The countryside was stocked. Ten barrels of gunpowder could set off more than half a million musket shots.

In the great war that followed, there would be no armed conflict in New Hampshire. But the gunpowder and the weaponry from Fort William and Mary made its way south to the battlefields, to aid the Patriot effort. Six months after the raid, in mid-June of 1775 as Minutemen assembled in the pastures and rolling land near Boston's Bunker Hill, they would send for some of that gunpowder, and it would serve to inflict hard damage upon the Royal Army. In two hours at the Battle of Bunker Hill, 226 British soldiers were killed and 828 were wounded, more than twice the number of casualties that the Patriots sustained.

What did Paul Revere do during the time of the sieges of Fort William and Mary? He kept the gray horse and stayed out on the assignment for five full days. He is not known to have been at the fort. But might he have been among those men as they gathered and planned? Did he spend his nights at the Portsmouth home of the Patriot leader John Sullivan, a home that Revere is known to have visited and where militia leaders convened before Sullivan led the second strike on the fort? Did Revere, as some have speculated, take a meal or more than one at the table of elderly Hunking Wentworth, uncle to the Royal governor but friend to the Patriot cause?

The weather had cleared and calmed, and the sun provided a touch of warmth on the days that Revere rode south, homebound on the Boston Post Road. By the time he returned to Boston, bringing news that he had delivered the message and that the mission to Fort William and Mary was complete, Joshua would be ten days old.

It might be argued with some reason that indeed it was here, in a parish of Portsmouth, New Hampshire, that the Revolutionary War began. Here at Fort William and Mary, where Royal soldiers fired shots at a Patriot militia for the first time and from whose stores the rebels armed themselves for the earth-shifting battles ahead. Given all that it engendered, was this the ride of Paul Revere's that launched America's rebellion past the point of no return?

Reverend Jonas Clarke's house, today

8

THE SUNDAY BEFORE

SUNDAY, APRIL 16, 1775

IN THE MORNING, AND IT WAS EASTER MORNING, Revere left his home in the North End and found a way to get himself out of Boston and then mounted a horse and rode away from the city, past the homes in Charlestown and Cambridge and out over the rutted spring roads and dewy pastures toward Lexington. Farmlands sprung alive on such mornings, piglets underfoot of the hogs, cows lowing for their calves, geese honking overhead. In many of the houses—in Medford, in Menotomy—breakfast sat on the fire and the family dressed for church. Revere would have no cause to stop along his way. He moved at a gallop when the route allowed.

He might have slipped out across the river by rowboat before daybreak or somehow else eluded the scores of redcoats who kept Boston under watch. He'd been heavily marked by the British Regulars ever since his ride to Portsmouth a few months before. He'd been marked for much longer than that, but after Portsmouth, especially. For the British, Revere being out on a mission usually meant trouble.

Possibly Revere had a friend on the loyalist side who helped him get out of the city that Easter morning. Revere knew people: friends, acquaintances, and business customers on both sides of the nascent conflict. Some of the Boston Masons who were in the employ of the Crown might nonetheless have been bound by a loyalty to the Masonic brotherhood, and to the brotherhood's value of secrecy, when the opportunity came to aid Revere as he sought to leave the city.

For the better part of a month Samuel Adams and John Hancock—the brains and the financial ballast of the Revolution respectively—had been staying in Lexington, at the home of the Reverend Jonas Clarke. And that is where Revere was bound this morning. Boston was no longer safe for Adams and Hancock. Vandals sometimes damaged Hancock's mansion on Beacon Street, and rogue loyalists could be inclined to hector or accost either man. More than four thousand redcoats were in a city with sixteen thousand residents, and at any time General Gage might have had either Adams or Hancock or both arrested on grounds of treason. Another Royal general surely would have. King George III had made it clear that Samuel Adams and John Hancock, enemies to the Crown's intent, were to be forcibly apprehended and taken into British control.

To be in Lexington gave Adams and Hancock a place of relative refuge and also placed them near to where the Provincial Congress met, one town over in Concord. Reverend Clarke's home sat just off the road that came into Lexington from the north. Since the time Adams and Hancock had arrived, members of the local militia had watched the house protectively.

A general state of nervous anticipation, a tension and uncertainty, blanketed Lexington and Concord and Menotomy and all the towns in the area. The British Regulars might at any instant move to take possession and command of the resources in the province. More than a week before, Revere had himself ridden to Concord—quickly in and quickly out—to warn that the supplies there could be at risk and should be moved. Those Concord stores held what was needed for battle and for sustenance. Gunpowder and fieldpieces. Cannon, balls, bullets, silver, long knives, flour, butter, salted beef and salted fish, rice, tea, raisins, rum and wine. Tents, hatchets, pickaxes, and sackcloth. Helves. Medical supplies. Materials for building barracks.

The Minutemen had taken to bringing their guns and bayonets with them to the tavern, to the market, to town meetings, even to church, lest they be suddenly called upon. Along with the Minutemen, the ordinary men of the towns—the many farmers, the clockmakers, the carpenters—kept their personal weapons cleaned and prepared. Many of those locals held at the ready a ration of food and ammunition, enough for a day of battle.

Clarke's home—large, accessible, and many roomed—functioned like a parsonage. It stood near the meetinghouse, and parishioners often came to visit and to talk with one another and with Clarke, and his wife, Lucy. But it wasn't technically a parsonage. Clarke had bought the house and the farmland surrounding it many years earlier from Thomas Hancock, who was an uncle to John Hancock. The house had been built in 1737, and John Hancock himself had lived there during his childhood in the 1740s and 1750s. In those days, servants and enslaved people worked in the house. Thomas Hancock was a wealthy merchant and among his many business relationships he had connections to people involved in the trading of enslaved people. John Hancock's father (Thomas's brother) was dead, and Thomas and his wife, Lydia, had no children. John became like a son to them.

Now Hancock and Samuel Adams were staying at the house. They shared a bed in a corner room on the ground floor. A mirror hung above the chest of drawers. The window next to the writing table looked out toward the Lexington Green. Hancock's valet slept each night on the floor nearer to the hearth. Hancock's carriage driver slept out in the barn. Hancock's assistant, John Lowell, had a room at the Buckman Tavern nearby and with him a trunk filled with Hancock's papers. When John Hancock traveled, an entourage joined him.

Hancock's fiancée, Dorothy Quincy, was also at the house in Lexington, as was Hancock's aunt Lydia, and the two women slept in a room directly above Sam Adams and John Hancock. From that higher vantage point, looking out over the open farmland, Lexington Green was clearly visible, perhaps four hundred yards from the Clarkes' house. Reverend Clarke's office also occupied a room on that second floor, and alongside his office lay a warren of irregular, low-ceilinged rooms and nooks, where nine of his and Lucy's children slept. "Jonas, Mary, Betsy," Reverend Clarke would call out each morning, rousing them. "William, Peter, Lucy, Lydia . . ."

In April of 1775, the Clarke children ran in age from five months to fifteen years old. They played marbles and games of tic-tac-toe and dressed up dolls made from corn husks. They helped work the farm and do household chores. In that crowded house the kitchen and the parlor and all the main rooms bustled throughout the day. There might be someone churning butter and someone else spinning thread on the wheel. Someone tending to a roast or someone letting in a parishioner or other visitor through the front door and onto the landing by the foot of the stairs.

At the side door, herb seedlings filled the soil of the kitchen garden. Apple mint, bee balm, dill, houseleek. Lavender. Rue and rosemary. Sorrel, feverfew, and thyme. Fellow preachers who stopped in to see the Clarkes came for discussions about God and farming and, now more than ever, about society, government, and politics. They came for the warmth of the home, as well as for a good meal. On April 15, the Reverend Samuel Cooper of Boston's Congregational Brattle Street Church—where Hancock and Sam Adams, as well as John Adams and Joseph Warren, attended—ate dinner at the Clarkes' house in Lexington. The next morning Reverend Cooper led the Sunday service in Sudbury, fifteen miles down the road. Many of the churches in this part of Massachusetts Bay were Congregational, not tied to the Church of England, and full of Patriotic sentiment.

Jonas Clarke had been preaching in Lexington for close to twenty years by this time, a figure woven into the community who on Sundays presided masterfully over the parishioners. Lexington was a town of maybe nine hundred people, and nearly as many cows. Reverend Clarke tended to his own crops and livestock and pitched his own hay, and when he preached, he used the simple language of the ordinary citizen. His sermons extended beyond an hour, sometimes well beyond. He waved his arms as he spoke, and when he touched on notions of individual liberty, and other Patriot values, he usually did so in nonspecific terms. "How can this lesson be used in your spiritual quest for salvation?" Revered Clarke would ask the congregation after stressing a point or reaching the end of a parable. Long, standing prayers preceded and followed the sermons. The Lexington meetinghouse was full on Sundays, the town around it quiet in that time.

Along the road Revere traveled to Lexington, he might, on a different spring day, have encountered any number of carriages laden with green vegetables, meat, butter, cheese, wood, molasses, ashes, dung. Farmers going to market. But on an Easter Sunday the carriages would be idle, and the horses at rest and the roads largely empty. Revere rode west through Menotomy and into Lexington along the road to Concord and then bore right and arrived at the Clarke house to spend some time with Samuel Adams and John Hancock.

It may be that Revere received some information from the two men that he then took with him back to Joseph Warren in Boston. Adams and Hancock had just adjourned a session of the Provincial Congress, which would have produced news. And Adams may have gotten some notice about the activity of the British Regulars from a source, whether sent by Margaret Kemble Gage, the British general's wife, or by another person with advance knowledge of troop movements.

The news that Revere had come to deliver, what he and Warren had been discussing before he left, was the unusual activity of the British troops around Boston. "The boats belonging to the transports are all launched and carried under the sterns of the men-of-war," Revere told Adams and Hancock that morning. Even more suspicious, Revere reported, was that suddenly the redcoat "grenadiers and light infantry were all taken off duty."

The British had meant this maneuver as a kind of disguise, a signal that they were relaxing in their vigilance. But it served as no disguise at all. It served as a tip. "From these movements," Revere would recall, "we expected something was to be transacted." A serious action on the part of the British Regulars now seemed imminent. Hancock sent word that any remaining stores still in Concord were to be removed and relocated. Quickly, they were, taken to outlying barns and into home cellars, hidden beneath pine boughs in the neighboring woods, buried in the working fields. Adams and Hancock were themselves now under fresh alert. From this moment the local militia watched over the Clarke House in even greater earnest, ready to defend its perimeter, to turn away any advancing redcoat or other figure of potential menace.

Revere would ride home that day and leave off his borrowed horse in Charlestown and stop to speak with a man he knew and get over the water and back to his home in the North End, his mission to Lexington fulfilled. The Reverend Jonas Clarke always kept a careful log of the visitors he had to his home, a log for posterity and for reference. Yet on that Sunday, April 16, 1775, he made no log entry mentioning the visit by Paul Revere. Recording it might have been risky had someone with British sympathies found it. And so, as far as anyone outside the Revolutionary leaders in Lexington knew, Paul Revere had never been to the Clarke house that Easter Sunday. He was never in Lexington that day at all.

WHEN HE CROSSED the river back into Boston that afternoon or evening of Sunday, April 16, 1775, Revere didn't know whether if soon called upon he would again be able to escape the city. The redcoats had their boots all over Boston. Samuel Adams and John Hancock were not alone in having departed their Boston homes. So had John Adams as well as many others prominent or conspicuous among the Patriot cause. The printer Isaiah Thomas was taking his press and his work out of town under threat of being arrested, or worse.

Revere, with his houseful of children, was for the moment holding his ground in the North End. So was Joseph Warren, the only prominent member of the Revolution's core leadership remaining in Boston by this time. Brave, stubborn, intrepid, strategic—some blend of all—Warren would be the linchpin on the inside.

Already it was tricky for a marked Patriot to slip out of Boston. The boats were in the water and the southern land passage, the Neck, was heavily manned by British Regulars and fortified with guardhouses. The likelihood of an unpassable lockdown loomed. The rebel leaders, as Revere would years later recall, "were apprehensive," believing that in the case of a British mission being underway, "it would be difficult to cross the Charles or get over Boston Neck."

When Revere stopped off in Charlestown that afternoon or evening of April 16, he sought out a man of about his age, a man he knew and could trust—Colonel William Conant, a known and reliable Son of Liberty. Revere told Colonel Conant that a British action toward Lexington and Concord appeared at hand, and when it unfolded, there was a plan to alert the Minutemen and the villagers how, in what manner, the Regulars were proceeding. From the heart of Charlestown anyone could look toward Boston and see the spire of the Old North Church. Revere told Conant that he had conceived of a method of signaling: "That if the British went out by water, we would show two lanterns in the North Church steeple—and if by land, one."

Old North Church

9

BIDDEN

April 18, 1775

The sash windows of the bedroom where Paul Revere and Rachel Walker Revere slept faced east, toward the light of dawn and the glinting water and the sounds of the waterfront and the wharf a few hundred yards away. Revere had bought the house in the early months of 1770, moving there with his wife, Sarah, and their five surviving children. Sarah was again pregnant, and Paul's businesses had by that point prospered enough to allow him to secure and own a home. The rooms were large and the spacious attic was an added benefit. It was a good house in a good part of town. Revere agreed to a price of 213 pounds, 6 shillings, and 8 pence. He took a mortgage.

The front of the house ran right up against North Square. In back, a fair bit of land reached all the way across the block to Middle Street, and to the grounds of the New Brick Church. Revere had a small barn built on the property—to keep a cow, perhaps, possibly a mare, and to shelter chickens in a coop. Some of the backyard land Revere leased to a tenant. The main house, wooden, narrow-paneled along the sides, and rising to gabled roofs, had stood sturdy on its oak beams since 1680. The pinewood floorboards in the Reveres' bedroom and in other rooms of the house ran wider than the length of even a tall man's foot.

When Sarah died in the spring of 1773, Paul and the seven surviving children lived in the house along with Revere's mother, Deborah, who slept in a quieter bedroom toward the back and paid her son a regular rent. Later in 1773 Paul married Rachel Walker, and it was Rachel who bore the great effort of maintaining and operating the household in the years that Paul's political commitment grew, when he would on many evenings be out meeting with the Masons or with members of the North End Caucus at the Green Dragon Tavern or was somewhere else watching the movements of the redcoats. Other times

Paul might have been gone for days on end, having ridden horseback to deliver and gather information on behalf of Joseph Warren and the Patriot leaders. The ages of Revere's children spanned twelve years—four to sixteen—even before he and Rachel had their first in '74.

A gently curving staircase came down off Paul and Rachel's bedroom, twelve steps to the front hall, where the linens and house tools might have been stored and where Rachel had her favorite armchair. In the kitchen hung large cast-iron pots and smaller ones, and for much of each day water simmered in a pot over the fire. There were flat wooden surfaces along the sides of the room for cutting vegetables and kneading dough. Meat roasted on a small spit. Bread baked in the wood-fed oven. Scents drifted through the house. A long woodpile would have lain just outside the back door, fuel for the busy kitchen, and set back away from the busy, bustling streets around North Square: merchants, seamen, children, men and women, servants, enslaved men and women, orphans, toughs, artisans, and fops. French immigrants. Dutch immigrants. Whigs, Tories, and those who couldn't decide. Boston's tainted egalitarian mass.

On March 5, 1771, a little more than a year after Paul and Sarah had moved in and exactly one year after the Boston Massacre, Revere created a provocative, stunning, macabre commemoration of that event and displayed it through the ground-floor windows. "In the Evening there was a very Striking Exhibition at the Dwelling House of Mr. Paul Revere, fronting the Old North Square," the *Boston Gazette* reported later that month. The description would also appear elsewhere, in sister newspapers, including seven hundred miles south in the *Virginia Gazette* out of Williamsburg. One of Revere's windows featured a depiction of the bleeding ghost of Christopher Seider, a twelve-year-old boy who two weeks before the Boston Massacre had been killed by a customs officer—causing great outrage and a massive public funeral and leading in a way to the "massacre" itself. As the *Gazette*s had it:

> Seider, with one of his Fingers in the Wound, endeavouring to stop the Blood issuing therefrom; near him his Friends weeping; at a small Distance a monumental Pyramid, with his Name on the Top, and the names of those killed on the 5th of March—Crispus Attucks, James Caldwell, Patrick Carr, Samuel Gray and Samuel Maverick—round the Base.
>
> In the next Window, were represented the [British] Soldiers drawn up, firing on the People assembled before them; the dead on the Ground; and wounded falling, with the Blood running in Streams from their Wounds; over which was written FOUL PLAY. In the third Window was the Figure of a woman representing AMERICA, sitting on

> the Stump of a Tree, with a Staff in her Hand, and the Cap of Liberty on the Top thereof, one Foot on the Head of a Grenadier lying prostrate, her Finger pointing to the Tragedy.
>
> The Whole was so well executed that the Spectators, which amounted to some Thousands, were struck by solemn Silence and their Countenances covered with the Melancholy Gloom. At nine o'Clock the Bells tolled a doleful Peal, until ten; when the Exhibition was withdrawn, and the People all retired to their respective Habitations.

If at that time one knew nothing else of Paul Revere's political views and intentions—and there was of course much more to know—the display alone was enough to signal his enmity toward British rule, the depth of his distaste. Even then, years before Revere became the rebellion's most trusted and valuable express rider, the still-benevolent General Gage and the Crown's less forgiving watchdogs knew to have an eye on Paul Revere.

CLOUDS LAY OVER Boston on the morning of April 18, 1775, yielding an occasional, drizzling, almost-English rain. It was not yet five o'clock when the gray sky began to whiten, and light fell against the windows of Paul Revere's bedroom. It would be time to go down the curving staircase and begin the 14,717th day of his life. After this sunrise, this day, the twenty-four hours that would follow, Revere's life and legacy, his place in the world and his own sense of self, would never be the same. After these twenty-four hours, the course of American history would forever be changed.

A murmuring coursed through those bustling North End streets, the burbling sense of a threat, of a boot about to fall. That morning, General Gage dispatched some men out of Boston into the outlying roads and villages to patrol and stand sentinel. This would be additional security for when the redcoats embarked that night—fresh watches to thwart someone trying to get into the villages to alert and rally the Patriot militia, an express rider, that is, or "the noted Paul Revere," as a British regimental soldier would later refer to him when describing the night of the ride.

"A small party on horseback is ordered out to stop all advice of your March getting to Concord," Gage wrote to Lieutenant Colonel Francis Smith, who would lead the Regulars that night. The size and the gravity of what the British were undertaking was not lost on Gage. Nor was the risk, nor the conviction of the Patriots.

Despite his reluctance to take arms against the sea of rebels, Gage knew by now that taking arms was inevitable, the necessary consequence of the Townshend Acts and resistances, the pressures, and the defiance, of the previous year and years. "The die is now cast, the colonies must either submit or triumph," King George III had written to Lord North, England's prime minister, in the fall of 1774. This was in the wake of the Suffolk Resolves. "The New England governments are in a state of rebellion," the king added soon afterward. "Blows must decide whether they are to be subject to this country or independent."

In early 1775 the British Parliament passed a resolution allowing a pointed and barely ambiguous missive to be sent by England's secretary of state, Lord Dartmouth, to Gage in America. The letter left England in mid-March and arrived in Boston on April 14, and its purpose was clear: no more dithering, General Gage, it is time to enforce the power of the Crown.

Gage would have discretion in just how and where to take military action, but action was wanted and wanted soon. The "first and essential step," wrote Lord Dartmouth, was to at long last arrest the Provincial Congress's resistance leaders—John Hancock and Samuel Adams. Perhaps Joseph Warren, too. Further, Gage was to prepare for and embrace the likelihood of violence. Dartmouth noted that General Gage's own descriptions made it plain that the people of the New England colonies "show a determination . . . to commit themselves at all events in open rebellion. In such a situation force should be repelled by force."

Lord Dartmouth pledged more troops from England

in the coming months, though far fewer than General Gage hoped for. In early April two additional British sloops of war, the sixteen-gun *Nautilus* and the fourteen-gun *Falcon,* arrived at Boston Harbor.

All throughout the New England colonies people knew something was impending, that the conflict might soon come to a head. Away from Boston and its surrounding towns, however, away from Massachusetts Bay, there was an absence of urgency. Life continued naturally, with ordinary dedication and touched by the innocence of daily duty. In Rhode Island, on April 16, the Reverend Ezra Stiles performed a baptism and gave Communion. In New Hampshire, on the eighteenth, farmers sawed shingles and plowed their fields as the warm, rainy afternoon gave way to a clear, fair night. The bliss of quiet ignorance before the storm. It would be a day or two after the fact that the people in those farther New England towns would learn what had happened in Lexington and Concord.

By the evening of the eighteenth Gage's advance men, twenty in all, patrolled in Cambridge and Menotomy and along the road to Concord west of Boston. Gage still hoped for an efficient, unanticipated march by the Regulars, a bloodless mission to Concord and a surgical removal of the stores. He would send out eight hundred redcoats toward Concord that night, foot soldiers led by Lieutenant Colonel Smith and Major John Pitcairn, who quartered at the Shaws' house beside the Reveres'. Gage never did give the order to arrest John Hancock and Samuel Adams. He urged his Regulars to show restraint and to treat the Patriots fairly and without unnecessary malice. The soldiers should not, Gage wrote to Lieutenant Colonel Smith, "plunder the Inhabitants, or hurt private property." Gage did not want the soldiers to open fire, but of course he knew they might. To the end General Gage was hoping against hope that nothing would go awry.

THE RAIN SLACKENED further. The showers grew more sporadic, then stopped. The British troops, having been told they would soon be put to action, set about their preparations, busying around Boston like birds ahead of the coming squall. Longboats were brought in close to their mother ships. Redcoats walking the city's inner streets strode out to the ends of the piers to huddle and talk. British sailors came off their boats and into town and spoke loosely of what was to come. "There'll be hell to pay tomorrow," said one soldier to another at a livery stable near the Province House, the Royal governor's mansion. When a young man—a friend of liberty—relayed that overheard comment to Revere and suggested it meant that the British would soon be on the march, Revere answered, "You are the third person who has brought me the same information." Later in the day, as Revere would recall, “It was observed that a number of soldiers were marching towards the bottom of the Common.” To get into position, that is, to cross the water to Charlestown or to the Cambridge shore.

While the Regulars knew that they were soon to engage, most did not yet know the specific intentions of their mission. But some did. Gage had earlier outlined the plan in secrecy to Lord Hugh Percy, a confidant and a general in the Royal Army. Then on that day, the eighteenth, Gage had written out instructions for the mission to its commander, Lieutenant Colonel Francis Smith. Tightly held information. And yet when Percy arrived, in mufti and unrecognized, and joined a crowd of Bostonians watching the assemblage of Regulars at the Common, he heard someone in the crowd say, “The British troops have marched, but will miss their aim.”

Percy asked, “What aim?”

And the answer: “The cannon at Concord.”

This was part of what led Lord Percy and General Gage to suspect a leak, a betrayal from their inner circle. By now, in Boston, word was out.

Revere did not know it, but by late afternoon Gage’s lookout men were long since over the Neck and out onto the roads west of Boston, finding their positions. The clouds were gone, and the misting ended. The sun sank below the hills of Cambridge, beyond the farmlands and beyond the Lexington Green and the road to Concord. The moon rose just above the water, and the clear night sky began to take its early shape. The Regulars were moving, quietly now and softly, in small groups toward the waterfront. Each soldier had a day's provisions in a haversack. They'd been told to leave their larger knapsacks behind.

And then, as Revere wrote in his first description of the events of April 18, 1775—a description he conveyed in a deposition to the Massachusetts Provincial Congress later that same year, then echoed for the historian Jeremy Belknap two decades later, "I was sent for by Dr. Joseph Warren about 10 o'clock that evening." Warren, Revere added, sent for him "in great haste."

WARREN RENTED A spacious family home on Hannover Street, a wide road west of North Square and off the southern edge of Mill Pond. Six double-hung sash windows ran across the second story of the house, five across the ground floor. Two strong chimneys, good headroom in the attic, a fruit tree in the front yard. Warren kept his medical office here, too, and his apprentice, William Eustis, who was twenty-one years old and newly out of Harvard, lived with him. Given the medical office, and Warren's openness to treating anyone in need—Whig,

Tory, white, Black, moneyed or not—people might come and go much more often and thus less conspicuously than to an ordinary home.

Within the Crown's steadily tightening grip on Boston, Warren's house had become a kind of internal nerve center for the Revolution, and a hub for the growing spy network that delivered notice and detail of redcoat activity. A spy might simply be a friend to the cause or just as likely a paid informer otherwise engaged in a common job—a tanner, a smith, a stable hand. They were people who worked in public places where things could be overheard. The best of the informers were quiet and easily overlooked, friendly enough, accommodating to most anyone, showing no political loyalty, no conspicuous leaning either way.

In the sitting rooms Warren kept Madeira and Lisbon wine. Among his many collected paintings hung portraits by John Singleton Copley of Warren and of Warren's wife, Elizabeth, who had died in 1773. Also, a mahogany eight-day clock ticked grandly against the wall, adorned with an inscription in Latin, *Ut Hora Sic Vita Transit,* "Life flies as the hour passes."

A four-minute walk from Warren's house was the Green Dragon Tavern, where in the early 1770s much of the assembled discussion and planning around acts of resistance unfolded. Four minutes, or half that time on a run. General Gage's Royal headquarters at the Province House stood slightly farther off, operating maybe half a mile from Warren's home.

Earlier in April Warren had arranged for his fiancée, Mercy Scollay, and his four children to leave Hannover Street and go live more safely outside Boston. The children ran in age from three to nine and were Warren's children with Elizabeth. Now Scollay looked after them with a motherly attentiveness. By the night of April 18, she and the children were fifty miles away in Worcester. Warren was home.

The light from the low moon had not yet come over the tops of the houses and buildings of the North End as Revere, now bidden, set out for Warren's house. Darkness lay over the town. Revere had visited Warren so often over the recent years. For business. For talk. For tea. Revere would go out from his house onto North Street and cut over on Gallop's Alley, dark and narrow. Revere was broad at the shoulders and tended to swing his arms, and the alleyway was less than five feet across. Down Middle Street then, past the Three Crowns, past the corners of Cross Street and then the wider stretches of Centre Street, and Mill Creek, until Hannover Street began. Revere moved in haste, but also quietly, carefully, remaining undetected. The darkness helped.

Some noise came from the taverns, but not much. Dim lamplight glowed here or there, though most of the windows in the homes were dark. A door closing somewhere, the rustle of a small animal along the soggy edges of the road, a clatter from someone's kitchen, a dog's bark—these small intrusions into the quiet night. The Regulars had begun to muster along the western shore, farther away on the far side of Warren's house.

Revere had walked these streets many thousands of times. Walked, run, skipped, hopped, limped. He'd met friends along these streets and business partners and co-conspirators. He had laughed on these streets, whispered and shouted on them, quarreled and fought. He had on these streets felt the freedom of younger days and felt the churn of his own ambition. Here Revere had plotted with a Son of Liberty. There he had met with someone about a bit of extra work. He had strolled on these streets with Sarah and with Rachel and with his parents. The streets of Revere's entire life, and now the streets where his son Paul and his other children made their daily way. These were streets and paths and alleyways, corners and bends, that Revere knew as well as any man alive. Moonlight, no moonlight, the full blackness of the narrowest way, no matter. Blind, he could have found Warren's front door.

Revere knocked and went inside. He would remember what Warren said to him until the day he died. "He desired me to go to Lexington and inform Mr. Samuel Adams and the Hon. John Hancock Esq. that there was a number of Soldiers, composed of Light troops and Grenadiers marching to the bottom of the Common, where there was a number of Boats to receive them," Revere recalled. "It was supposed that they were going to Lexington, by way of Watertown to take them, Mess. Adams and Hancock, or go to Concord."

William Dawes

10

THE ESTIMABLE WILLIAM DAWES

WARREN DISPATCHED REVERE TO LEAVE THE city across the river to Charlestown. It made sense. That's the way Revere tended to go rather than work through the city streets and try to leave over land from the south. Revere kept a rowboat hidden among some brush along the North End shore, east of the Charlestown Ferry. But getting across would not be easy—not with the way the river was manned and with the redcoats being on heightened alert. More than ever there loomed a likelihood that Revere could get stopped and taken in. Warren knew that, they all did, which is why when Revere arrived at Warren's house he learned that Warren had also enlisted a second rider to go alert Samuel Adams and John Hancock, insurance in case the British thwarted Revere. "I found he had sent an express by land to Lexington," Revere recalled. "A Mr. William Dawes."

Dawes was to leave Boston by land, to go south over Boston Neck and through the teeth of the Royal guards.

If Revere had made his way to the front lines of the rebellion from outside the favored class, winning respect and stature through his hard work and ingenuity, his drive and his social way, his Masonic presence and his smarts, Dawes had been born into much more immediate prominence, from a deeply entrenched family line. Revere was the son of a French immigrant who'd landed in Massachusetts Bay just sixty years before the spring of 1775. Dawes's great-great-great-grandfather, also William Dawes, had sailed over from Sudbury, England, in the 1620s, at the very dawn of the colony. A Dawes had lived near the heart of Boston for most of the fifteen decades since. They came from exceptional wealth in England, and they continued to prosper in the new land, securing a mansion on one of Boston's earliest streets. In the 1660s members of the Dawes family helped to both found and to build the Old South Church, which broke away from Boston's First Church in religious defiance. A history of architecture and skilled masonry ran in the family. In the 1770s Thomas

Dawes, a peer and first cousin to William Dawes, designed the Boston State House and the Brattle Street Church and built Hollis Hall at Harvard. Both Thomas and William were active Patriots—in William's case often craftily—as was William's father, who was also named William. John Adams, speaking with Samuel Adams, described the Daweses as one of the most "noble families to rise up in Boston."

Among those engaged in the resistance to British rule, few were more pedigreed or long tied to the land than William Dawes. He was thirty years old on the night of the Ride, a full decade younger than Revere. He had money. And he carried his family name wherever he went.

THE SHIP THAT first brought the Dawes family from England to the New World sailed under the guidance of John Endicott, a Puritan who had been commissioned by a King's Council to stake and develop ground for settlers. The ship came to shore on the pierless, wharfless wilds of Salem on September 6, 1628. In the decades that followed, as the colony formed and more settlers arrived and a government began to take shape, the Great and General Court of Massachusetts Bay established what would become known as the Ancient and Honorable Artillery Company of Massachusetts. This served as the closest thing the colonists had to a local army, and the Artillery Company outlined its purpose: "to train and exercise in military discipline and in the use and care of military weapons and equipment." Later, the Artillery Company designated 30 percent of its membership, to "be ready at half an hour's warning upon any service they shall be put to by their military officer." These were the forebears of the Minutemen, who were indeed ready on short warning when they were roused by Revere and other alerts on the night of April 18, 1775.

To this day great pride endures among those in the Dawes lineage. Much of the family's story is presented in books created by Dawes descendants: *William Dawes and His Ride with Paul Revere,* published in 1878 by Henry Ware Holland, and *A Bicentennial History of the Midnight Ride, April 18–19, 1775, of William Dawes, First Rider for Revolution, a "Chronological Narrative"* complied by C. Burr Dawes and published in 1976.

The Dawes who stood out and distinguished himself in the Ancient and Honorable Artillery Company was William's great-grandfather Ambrose Dawes, who joined the company in 1674. The next year Ambrose fought as a lieutenant in King Philip's War, in which colonists and some indigenous allies fought against a large faction of indigenous peoples in northern New England. This brutal war lasted close to three years. Many towns were destroyed, and thousands of indigenous people and colonists died. The conflict is notable because the colonist soldiers, Ambrose Dawes among them, received no aid from the

British or any other European country. Some have called King Philip's War the first American war.

Ambrose Dawes remained an active, respected member of the military, known for his commitment and cited for his courage. In 1692, during a skirmish with indigenous people over a fort in Maine, he lost an eye, ending his military career. Many years later, in 1735 as part of a compensatory act, Ambrose's son Thomas, the grandfather of William, was allotted more land in posthumous recognition of Ambrose's outstanding service. Over time Thomas and his wife, Sarah, grew their wealth. They owned and passed along to their survivors the family mansion on Sudbury Street—which ran along the eastern edge of Boston's West End—as well as three other nearby homes, some pastureland, and additional property.

With this heritage and into this wealth and social standing William Dawes, rider for the Revolution, was born on April 6, 1745. His father ran a prosperous tailoring shop on Salt Lane just north of the family's home, on a plot of land nearer to the wharves. William was one of nine children, and the eldest son. When he was sixteen, his mother died during childbirth.

Despondent at the loss of his wife, William's father left his work and moved the family to a farm in Marlborough, thirty miles west of the city. There were numerous chores to be done around the house and on the farmland, and because his father was physically limited by a clubfoot, much of that chore work fell to the younger, physically robust William. Earlier he had helped his father at the tailor shop. According to the narrative compiled by C. Burr Dawes, William's father took life seriously and held to religious observance. The family prepared meals ahead of the Sabbath, so that the day could be observed as one of true rest, and on those Sabbath days William's father forbade his children to laugh or to look out the window.

William worked to help and support the family, and although his schooling ended early, his exposure to learning did not. His grandfather on his maternal side, the printer and bookseller Nicholas Boone, had produced dozens of books and sold hundreds more. Many volumes stayed in the family. Religious tracts and military texts. Almanacs. Medical reviews. Books about pirates. Dawes grew up reading a lot.

Tall, broad shouldered, and genial, Dawes soon came into his own trade, as a tanner. Not long after that, in 1768 at age twenty-three, he married Mehitable May—nineteen years old, vivacious, capable, beautiful, and the daughter of a wealthy carpenter. In the 1630s the May family had helped establish the town of Roxbury, just over the Boston line. In her portrait Mehitable wears a tall hat with a luxuriant bow and a blue dress cut low at the neck. A lush tress of her hair rests upon her shoulder.

The couple showed great affection for each other, and others marked them for their good humor and their obvious enjoyment of life. They wed at Old South Church, the same church that William's great-great-grandfather and great-grandfather had helped to found and build a hundred years before. This was a time in Boston when staunch Patriots, angered by the Townshend Acts, were loath to buy goods imported from England. On his wedding day, Dawes, as the pro-Patriot *Boston Gazette* reported approvingly, "dress'd wholly in the Manufactures of this Country, wherein he did honor to Himself, and merits the respect of his Province."

William and Mehitable lived on Ann Street, a short stretch from the home of William's father, now remarried, back in Boston, and a successful blacksmith. The younger William could leave through his backyard, cross a short bridge, and arrive at an entrance to Faneuil Hall, where the Ancient and Honorable Artillery Company met and trained. Dawes was now a member, as was his father and his cousin Thomas. On training days and for meetings, Dawes wore the official, handsome blue ensemble of the company, and he participated in larger, pompous ceremonies such as the June celebration of the birthday of King George III or the welcoming back to Boston of General Gage after his leave of absence in London. The members of the Artillery Company were naturally dressed in full uniform on such days. They would gather near Boston Common and select certain arms from the gun house—muskets or cannons—to fire in lusty salute. All through those tense years right up until the autumn of 1774, loyalists and Patriots of the Ancient and Honorable Artillery Company trained and marched and performed side by side with one another. They bonded through military exercise as they had bonded ever since the founding of the company. Among loyalists and Patriots there remained, even within the widening and increasingly febrile dissent, a common ground.

Although there were fierce loyalists within the wider Dawes family, William and his father's Patriot allegiances proved unambiguous. In December of 1773, his father's blacksmith apprentices boarded the anchored British ships and helped throw the tea into Boston Harbor. Afterward they convened at the elder Dawes's shop with tea leaves still lodged in the brims of their caps.

In 1773 or 1774 Dawes joined the Committee of Correspondence, which meant that he sometimes needed to go in and out of Boston to deliver messages or try to recruit allies to the Patriot cause. His easiest path out of the city went over Boston Neck. For one thing Mehitable's parents lived near there on land plenty big enough to keep a horse.

Yet the Neck, guarded tightly by redcoats, could be difficult to cross for anyone known and recognized as a Patriot. The land there was only 120 feet wide at high tide, and off its southern end, just outside the city bounds, remained an old scaffold erected in the 1600s for public executions. "Go ahead, Warren, you'll soon come to the gallows," a British officer once snarled at Dr. Joseph Warren while letting him pass to attend to a housebound patient.

Dawes was nowhere near as recognizable nor as influential as Warren, but he knew that, as he was a member of the Boston militia, it would be dangerous to go earnestly past the guards at Boston Neck on anything more than rare occasions. He wanted a disguise or deflection. He wanted to appear nonthreatening. And so, as his granddaughter later described it, "During these rides, he sometimes borrowed a friendly miller's hat and clothes and he sometimes borrowed the dress of a farmer and had a bag of meal behind his back on his horse." At times Dawes feigned drunkenness as well, slurring his speech, ambling happily and haphazardly on his horse, even coyly slipping a flask of metheglin—a kind of honey wine—to a soldier on guard. Other times at a nearby tavern frequented by British soldiers he'd slump over, feigning drunkenness again, as a way to eavesdrop on what the soldiers said.

That persona, of the jolly, intemperate Billy Dawes, was an act. Dawes's distaste for the British, and for the British forces crowding into Boston life, was sharp and real—at once philosophical, practical, and personal. One evening a half year into their marriage, Dawes and Mehitable were walking through Boston at dusk. Dawes and a friend had moved slightly in front of Mehitable when suddenly a British soldier stepped out and grabbed her and tried to carry her away. Mehitable was a small woman, but William Dawes was not a small man. When he saw what had happened, Dawes set upon the British soldier, freed his wife, and then, as C. Burr Dawes relates it, gave the soldier "a beating as sound as it was well deserved."

IN EARLY OCTOBER of 1774 the Ancient and Honorable Artillery Company completed its final exercises of the year. By spring the Revolutionary War would be underway. Tories and Whigs would never again consort in military activity in such a way as they had in the Artillery Company. Dawes, like others prominent in the company, knew something about the gun house on Boston Common. He knew how to get into it, for one thing, and he knew how it was guarded—and precisely when it was briefly left *un*guarded during roll call. Dawes also knew just what was inside the gun house, in particular two brass cannons, three-pounders, that the Patriots had a mind to take for their own. They were powerful enough to be formidable in battle, yet small enough for a clutch of strong men to carry off. These ideas set the stage for the most significant act of resistance William Dawes would ever commit.

The cannons came from England—the colonists were still two years from having the ability to forge such weapons on American soil. Each cannon was a phallic shaft of brass, four feet long, weighing 450 pounds, and ferocious in its capacity as a weapon of war. A horse towed it onto the battlefield, and six soldiers worked together to fire it safely. A three-pound cast-iron cannonball could decimate a man, or two, standing half a mile away. The cannons could also fire grapeshot and chain shot, the halves of a split cannonball joined by a chain. The halves would spread open in flight and hurtle wildly through the air, destroying or violently wounding whatever and whomever the projectile passed. Except at close range, the cannons were highly inaccurate.

And so, the heist: One afternoon while the guards were out on roll call, a team led by Dawes slipped into the gun house and removed the cannons out the back door—shielded in part by an accomplice's horses—and into a next-door schoolhouse. There the cannons remained, in a wooden box beneath a desk, literally underfoot of the schoolmaster. When a British sergeant arrived at the gun house and discovered the cannons were missing, he chastised the lieutenant in charge, "These fellows will steal the fillings out of your head while you are keeping guard."

After several weeks, the Patriots' Committee of Safety called upon Dawes to deliver the cannons to an outlying militia. As Henry Ware Holland recalls, "They were sent by boat to Waltham, and were in active service during the war."

During the removal of the heavy cannons Dawes sustained an injury, "his sleeve button getting embedded in his wrist," as his daughter, Mehitable, described it. "For some days he did not venture to seek surgical aid lest suspicion should at once attach him" to the theft. But the pain increased, and one night Dawes stole quietly from his home and went to see Joseph Warren. There was no hiding how he had gotten the wound, but Dawes stayed mum. "You are right not to tell me," said Dr. Warren as he treated him. "I had better not know."

Yet Warren did know what Dawes had done. And knew, too, of Dawes's playacting as he worked through the guards at Boston Neck. And so, when on April 18 it came time for Warren to select someone to ride out to Lexington, someone in addition to Paul Revere, Warren knew just whom to ask.

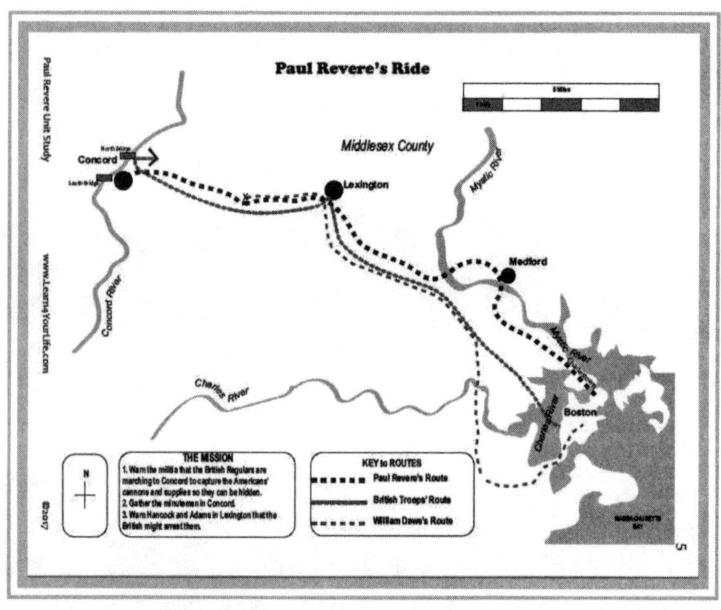

The routes of Revere, Dawes, and the British troops

II

THE RIDE

Revere left Warren's house, out the double front doors and down the few steps into the yard, and began to make his way back toward the North End. He would need to stop at home before beginning his mission to Lexington. First, he needed to stop somewhere else.

He walked along Hannover Street with the dark, still waters of Mill Pond a few hundred feet to his left, and the rustling of the narrow nighttime North End streets ahead of him. He passed the Green Dragon Tavern, where he had gone on so many nights over the years and been warmed by the wood burning in the hearth and smelled the grease lamps and sat looking across the table at other men in the resistance. Everyone involved understood the size of this collective venture—to make their own lives matter, and to give to the future a kind of societal liberty they had never known. All of those meetings and those nights had led up to this one.

Revere walked on for a while holding the knowledge of the assignment that lay before him, and aware of the sound of his footfalls on the soft ground. Soon he came to the home of Captain John Pulling, Jr.

Pulling was two years younger than Revere and they had known each other since childhood. Growing up, Pulling attended the Old North Church, Christ Church, as a parishioner during the same years that Revere rang the bells there. They had lived within the same web of streets all their lives and had gone to schools in the town. In the early 1770s both men were among the leadership of the North End Caucus, a Patriot political organization that played an active role in planning the initiatives and responses against British rule. Pulling still maintained a close attachment to the Old North Church. He was a vestryman.

"I left Doctor Warren, called upon a friend, and desired him to make the signals" is how Revere recalled it, sparing Pulling's name. Even as Revere neared Pulling's house, and as Dawes was preparing himself to cross over at Boston Neck, some eight hundred British soldiers were being ferried in small groups off the western shore of Boston, to Cambridge. There was no question how many lanterns Revere would tell Pulling to show in the steeple of the Old North Church. Two. The British had gone out by water.

REVERE LEFT PULLING and went back home, to steal quietly into the hall, pull on an overcoat, and get into his riding boots. Revere did not take his flintlock pistol. There were soldiers in the streets of Boston and there might be soldiers at any point on his journey—Revere could guess that much. Gage's advance men were by now stationed throughout the countryside, in twos and fours and sixes, waiting in hollows and swales and tree-covered paths off the larger roads. Even unarmed there was a chance Revere would be killed. If he had a pistol on him, that chance would be greater still. Revere secured his boots. Heavy, and straight along the inner sole, the boots ran to the top of Revere's calves and fastened by button onto his buckskin pants. He said goodbye to Rachel and then again stepped out into the night. "I went to the north part of town where I kept a boat," Revere said later.

He would have come off Charter and onto Henchman, or onto slender Foster Lane, just twelve feet wide with houses on either side, a gentle slope down to a stretch of flatland, and then the shore. There may have been some stirring in the side alleys to the left or the right of him or it may have been mostly quiet. Revere was around the bend and out of sight from the Charlestown Ferry landing.

Moonlight touched the water, and so did some light from the lamps of the *Somerset* man-of-war. The river moved quietly. All the smaller boats had been drawn up alongside the warships, and men were meant to be out on the ship decks keeping watch: no one was allowed to cross. The western shore, where the redcoats were crossing boat by boat to Cambridge, was not at all near to where Revere stood.

Revere's rowboat lay hidden along the shore beneath an old, tattered wharf. He had enlisted two friends, two Patriots, to row him across. Joshua Bentley was forty-eight years old and made his living as a boatbuilder. He had a son attending Harvard. The other rower was a shipwright with the last name of Richardson. This was not, to put it mildly, a safe time to cross the river. But the moon would only rise higher behind them as the night went on, and Revere needed to be quickly on his way, and there was no reason to think there would be any better time to make the crossing that night. Now was the time to push off.

WITH THE INSTRUCTIONS from Revere, John Pulling left his house and went to the home of Robert Newman, the sexton of the Old North Church. Newman lived with his mother and his stepfather on Salem Street, maybe thirty paces from the church on the opposite side. They had taken in British boarders as a source of income, and the boarders were home playing cards at the table that night. Newman was twenty-three years old, fifteen years younger than Pulling, and Newman had the keys to open the great wooden door at the front of the church.

Newman slipped out of the house and into the yard—the same yard of his youth, where he had played boyhood games—and then joined with Pulling on the street. Another man, Thomas Barnard, midthirties, had engaged himself as well to keep an eye out for Royal soldiers. The men walked toward the church and carefully went inside. If they were quiet and quick, they could proceed without trouble. There was no reason for the redcoats to suspect subversive activity at the Old North Church that night.

The steeple stood 175 feet up from the ground, the crown atop the thick square tower that Newman knew intimately. He knew all the church's particulars, its nooks and recesses, its cracks, and stains, and beams, the weakened rungs on any ladder. That's a sexton's job. To know the grounds and the building. To keep the pews and pulpit clean after a service. To dry the rainwater in the belfry after a storm. To clean up after the pigeons roosting in the tower. As a rule, Newman kept to himself. He didn't talk much to anyone. He'd taken the job as sexton purely out of financial need.

Well before nightfall, Pulling and Newman had known by way of Revere that this moment of giving the signal would soon come. Two lanterns were already cleaned, freshly wicked, and at the ready in a closet near the stairs leading to the steeple. Newman was fit, nimble, and physically active in his life and work.

He wound his way up the twenty-four stairs to the library, to where the vestry office was, and then another twenty-eight stairs to the bell ringers' room. He strapped the lanterns onto a thick leather thong that he draped over the back of his neck—a lantern now hung on either side of him, his hands free for the climb. Newman carried flints and a tinderbox as well.

He continued now, hand over hand, on the mounted ladders, the wooden rungs, to the belfry itself—the housing of the eight great bells that Paul Revere had rung as a change ringer a quarter century before. Usually, to check on the bells, and sweep the landings, Newman made this ascent during the daytime. It was dark now, lightless save for some moonlight that came softly through the cracks in the tower, and the richer moonlight above at the top of the climb shining in through the steeple windows. The belfry was not even halfway up the tower. Ladders, landings, ladders, straight upward for another ninety feet or more. Even for Newman it proved difficult to know in the near darkness just how high he had reached, or how far a fall lay below him. Just as well. There was no point looking down.

Newman could hear pigeons cooing, then rustling as he ascended, the birds visible as shapes of shade above him. The lanterns swung at his sides. Shortly before the steeple, maybe twenty-five feet below, the tower featured large, imperfectly shuttered, and paneless windows, through which the wind blew, sending a chill and a hollow, rushing sound into the dark space. Then, as he climbed above that, the air was still again.

From the steeple chamber, Newman could look across the water to Charlestown. He could see the tops of the buildings in the North End and in other parts of Boston. Nearer to him, before the river, lay Copp's Hill Burying Grounds, dark and risen and planted with deciduous trees, its old mossy headstones now wrapped in silence.

The flint, the tinderbox, the ignited wick. First one, then the next. In the steeple window Newman briefly held the lighted lanterns together, then slowly spread them apart. He wanted to be as unambiguous as possible to someone watching from farther away: two points of light. Newman showed the lanterns for only moments, one minute, maybe two, but no more. His intention was that the Patriots on the far shore, in Charlestown, would see the lanterns, but he knew that others might see them as well, that others surely did see them. No other light like that was to be seen. Newman stood high above all else. Curfew had long since passed in locked-down Boston that night.

Now, after the showing of the lanterns, the church might no longer be safe for Newman, nor for anyone else. If the redcoats had seen or learned about these lantern signals, about such an act of opposition, of defiance, they would punish it.

Newman put out the lanterns and refastened them to the leather thong and again draped the thong over the back of his neck and began his hurried descent. Hand under hand, away from the light and back into the darkened tower. The one hundred and three rungs of the ladders. Then the fifty-two steps of the winding stairs to the floor of the church. He put away the lanterns, out of sight, and he and Pulling, waiting below with an eye on the door, got themselves out of the church, through a window at the back, to reach their homes before anyone saw them.

THE FIRST SETTLERS named the land there Meshaumul, "where there is a big river," and the river itself they called Quinobequin, a reference, in the language of the native Massachusett, to its meandering banks. The water wended wide, then narrow, then wide again, deeper waters into shallow marshes, briny and fertile, full of fish and fauna and creatures of the sea. Much later, in the early 1600s, the British named the river Charles after the son of their king. For thousands of years, the waterway, a tidal estuary off the infinite Atlantic, has been at the heart of a people's life and livelihood, and a place of passages to and from. The river is why Boston exists.

The three men got into the rowboat and pushed away from the old wharf. Revere kept his body low. Bentley and Richardson carefully dipped the wooden oars into the black water. At the point of the open rowlocks, on each side of the boat, they had wrapped the oar shafts in old clothing—a torn petticoat received from a woman who knew their cause—so as to muffle the knocking of their strokes in the quiet night. As they came farther away from the shore and toward the middle of the river bend, the three men could see the great HMS *Somerset* to the west, heaving on the rising tide, improbably large, her reflection rippling in the moonglow, her masts tall and ghostlike. A lion cathead came prominently off her bow.

Lantern light glowed from the *Somerset*'s decks. The lookouts, the Royal sailors and the Royal soldiers watching the river lest anyone pass, were stationed in light while Revere and Bentley and Richardson rowed in darkness. The rowboat may have been three hundred feet east of the *Somerset,* more or less. No one called out to them from the *Somerset,* no one shouted for the rowboat to stop. Bentley and Richardson pointed toward the nearest edge of the Charlestown Battery on the opposite shore. They rowed in the near silence, saying nothing. Long, even, quiet strokes, blades kept low to the surface, the boat's progress gently aided by the westward current.

How long did it take to cross that river? Ten minutes? Fifteen? Twenty-five? Did it seem like half the night? Revere felt the press of time, the intensity of what was at hand. He didn't know, nor would it have lessened his urgency, that the British troops were slow in getting themselves across the water. Too few boats for all those men. The long back-and-forth ferrying deposited small batches of soldiers on the far shore, leaving them there to stand by the river's edge and wait for more of their troops to arrive. The tide came in steadily, flooding the banks and dampening the soldiers' boots. The Regulars were crossing at a wider part of the Charles River than where Revere crossed, and the tide was pushing against them. They were poorly prepared.

Revere reached the Charlestown Battery and pulled himself out of the rowboat and stood on the Charlestown shore. In sixty days, British reinforcements would land near just this spot, arriving to fight in the bloody, fateful Battle of Bunker Hill. From where Revere now stood, he could look back across the water toward the Old North Church, clear against the star-salted, moonlit sky. It was nearly eleven o'clock. The signal lanterns, Revere would soon learn, had already appeared in the steeple.

The Old North Church had been a lodestar in the

North End of the city for all of Revere's life. A landmark of exceptional prominence. In April of 1760, when Revere was twenty-five and soldiers from America and Britain were still fighting side by side under the seal of the Crown, fighting France in the French and Indian War, members of the Old North Church illuminated its steeple in celebration of a Royal Army victory—the taking of Quebec from the French. Maybe the memory of that illumination is what had given Revere the idea to show the signal lanterns from there. It was the only logical place. So clear and high against the sky. At night, above the Old North Church, the moon would appear to the right of the steeple, and below the moon clouds sat above the waters of Boston Harbor, cloaking the harbor in mist.

Revere turned from the shoreline and walked toward the center of Charlestown. Plenty of loyalists lived among the Patriots here, but few soldiers were now about. "When I got into town, I met Colonel Conant and several others," Revere would recall. "They said they had seen our signals. I told them what was acting and went to get me a horse."

A horse needed to be first secured and then readied for Revere's ride. No one in Charlestown had known when he was coming, or whether he would come to Charlestown at all. No one might have imagined that Revere would get free of Boston. "While the horse was preparing," Revere remembered, "Richard Devens Esq., who was one of the Committee of Safety came to me and told me that as he came down the road from Lexington, after sundown that evening, he met nine officers of Gage's army, all well mounted and armed, going up the road towards Concord."

Devens had been traveling home by chaise from a committee meeting at a tavern in Menotomy. The British Regulars rode in a pack and had their servants with them. Seeing officers in the towns outside Boston was not unusual in those days, but to see them at that time of evening, riding away from their Boston encampments and traveling with clear intent, felt portentous.

Devens turned the chaise back to the tavern and delivered notice of what he'd seen to Elbridge Gerry, the committee leader. Gerry sent a message to John Hancock at the Reverend Jonas Clarke's house in Lexington, about five miles away. Gerry's message left the tavern by express rider around eight o'clock. About an hour later, Hancock sent a message back. "Dear Sir: I am much obliged for your notice. It is said the officers are gone to Concord, and I will send word thither. I am full with you that we ought to be serious, and I hope your decision will be effectual. I intend doing myself the pleasure of being with you tomorrow. My respects to the committee. I am your real friend, John Hancock."

Neither Hancock nor Gerry nor anyone in these towns outside Boston knew that hundreds of British soldiers were then crossing the Charles River, that a mission of such scale and promised violence had begun. They only knew—from this sighting of the officers on the road to Concord and from another sighting as well—that some disruption, likely to the coveted stores, seemed at hand. The presence of the officers whom Gage had earlier that day sent ahead to intercept Patriots from Boston proved, in precious irony, to be what alerted the Patriots to be in arms.

Revere, calm and eager, waited for his horse. The new knowledge that British officers riding good horses covered the roads ahead, and that these officers might corner him or fire at him, did not diminish Revere's resolution. Neither Devens nor Conant nor any of the other Whigs on the scene in Charlestown, now knowing the nature and the scope of Revere's mission, suggested they might ride with him and help to spread the alarm on the road to Lexington. As a rider and as a message bearer in a time of extreme duress, Revere was in a special class. "Steady, vigorous, sensible, and persevering," Thomas Young once said of Revere. Thomas Young was John Adams's family doctor, a member of the Committee of Correspondence, and an active Son of Liberty. "No man of his rank and opportunities in life deserves better of the community."

Other riders had been engaged and begun to disperse that night, and soon, alerted by Revere and by others, still more riders would spread out on routes that ran like so many veins through the body of land and people. It was Revere's natural reward to go this dangerous road to Lexington—an artery as it were, to the heart of it all—on horseback and alone.

Solomon Brown saw the officers, too, silhouetted on their mounts, riding ahead of him on the road to Lexington. They moved confidently and without haste, rattling gently in their saddles, their horses' hoofbeats muted by the soft, wet earth. Brown, returning home from market, rode up easily beside them. He was not two months past his eighteenth birthday. Deacon Brown's son. The soldiers wore blue overcoats now, and Brown, neither cowed nor troubled to see them, rode up alongside and then rode past. The road there lay narrower than it did elsewhere, the passing was close, and the men—the nine commissioned British soldiers riding with their servants, and the young man returning from market with his saddlebags—would acknowledge one another and have no conflict in the bluish nighttime light. They continued riding in this way, Brown drifting sometimes ahead and sometimes behind. A breeze blew, lifting the sides of the soldiers' overcoats, and then Brown could see the guns and the bayonets they were carrying.

Now he did ride out in front of them, casually still, so as not to seem alarmed, but without falling back. And then, as the road went on, he began to pull away. Brown lived a fair piece farther along, west of Lexington, in a house built just next to the wider road to Concord. But instead of going home he intended to first tell the people of Lexington what he had seen: Gage's men, in full arms.

Brown came into Lexington and rode up to the Munroe Tavern and there described the soldiers to William Munroe, the tavern owner. Munroe was twenty-three years old, and he was the first sergeant of the Lexington militia. "I supposed they had some design on Hancock and Adams," Munroe said. And so, Munroe summoned and posted additional guards around the perimeter of the Reverend Jonas Clarke's house, a group of eight men—armed, set, and primed. One of those eight men was William Munroe himself.

A mile on, Brown arrived at Buckman Tavern, the central gathering place of Lexington, the thriving, lively tavern where—during the hot and prescient years of the 1770s—Patriots so often convened to discuss ideas of the resistance and where members of the militia sought sustenance after training on the Lexington Green. Buckman Tavern, sturdy within its frame, sat just opposite the green at the place where the road to Concord crossed with the road that ran north and south through town. The tavern's upper floors afforded open views of both roads and in all directions. You could see into the surrounding farmland, and, more immediately, you could see the Lexington Meeting House and the home of the Reverend Jonas Clarke, where John Hancock and Samuel Adams now were.

Hancock's man, John Lowell, had rented a small room on the third floor of the Buckman Tavern, his sleeping mat tight beneath the slanted ceiling. The trunk in Lowell's care was full of Hancock's personal papers, including letters he had received and copies of letters he had sent. There would have been information about the Provincial Congress in Hancock's papers, and details of any number of Patriot plans. There would have been the names of critical rebels as well as the names of spies working for the Patriots and spies suspected of working for the British. From the Crown's perspective Hancock's trunk contained evidence of treason, many times over. Lowell understood that the trunk could not under any circumstances get into the hands of the Royal Army.

Buckman Tavern had drawn patrons in Lexington for more than half a century and flourished now under the ownership of Ruth and John Buckman—staunch Whigs. Things could really get going there, with food and Revolutionary talk luring and engaging the crowd. Ruth Buckman led the tavern kitchen, overseeing the cooks and the hearths, unveiling new foods, touching the dishes with garden-grown herbs—thyme, rosemary, and sage. Southernwood for the cakes. The Buckmans kept cows on their land, five of them. They churned their own butter and set their own cheese.

Nearly everyone in Lexington and the nearby towns had been to Buckman Tavern for something. Most people many times. Mail could be sent there and the Buckmans would hold it until its recipient came in. Local businesses—tanners, shoemakers, woodworkers—put up notice of their work on a post next to the bar. Overnight travelers made wayside layovers at Buckman Tavern or might stable a horse there and collect it a few days later. On Sundays, the churchgoers of Lexington came to Buckman Tavern before, after, or between the Reverend Jonas Clarke's sermons at the meetinghouse. Women and children populated the tavern rooms more conspicuously on those days, and the kitchen turned out plates of home-stuffed sausage, waffles, and eggs. Cups of hot chocolate.

On a weeknight such as Tuesday, April 18, 1775, the tavern might be full of men smoking clay pipes and drinking mugs of flip, the favored, hot concoction of rum, beer, egg, and molasses. The men sat or rocked on the maple chairs, put their hands upon the tables, checked their powder horns. Most everyone there had some part in the resistance, and the resistance flavored much of the talk in the air. The leading, most active Patriots would take to a side room to speak about things that were not to be widely known, seditious matters. It was here, in December of 1774, that town governors voted to provide bayonets for every Patriot soldier in training. If there was a public establishment in Lexington that a column of British Regulars might bully their way into, Buckman Tavern was it. John Buckman told Lowell he would keep Hancock's trunk under lock and key in the Buckmans' own bedroom. There was no safer place in the tavern.

Solomon Brown tied up his horse and walked into Buckman Tavern and told the people there about the British soldiers he had seen on the road. It must have been sometime after eight o'clock when Brown walked in. A tall wooden clock ticked against the wall of the meeting room on the second floor. Soon, the nine British soldiers would ride right through Lexington and a few other people would see them, too, moving so leisurely away from Boston at that time of night. "The unusually late hour of passing excited the attention of the citizens" is how Elijah Sanderson put it. Sanderson was twenty-three years old and lived right on the main road, less than a mile from the Lexington Green. "I took my gun and my cartridge box and, thinking something must be going on more than common, walked up to John Buckman's tavern."

What they knew in the tavern was only what they had seen: that armed Royal soldiers were out and present in the night and sauntering at an easy pace toward Concord. They knew nothing of the hundreds of British Regulars who were preparing to ferry across the Charles River.

Paul Revere had not yet begun to ride into the countryside.

Why were Gage's men—a solid clutch of them, though not nearly enough for a serious fight—out on horseback on this Tuesday night? What was their plan? They had not in passing through Lexington stopped to trouble or try to seize John Hancock or Samuel Adams. In the tavern the men decided that a few riders should follow the British soldiers to monitor them on their westward path: Elijah Sanderson, twenty-five-year-old Jonathan Loring, and the teenager who'd brought the news, Solomon Brown.

Sanderson borrowed a horse from another member of the militia. Brown also needed a horse. His was spent from the long day of traveling. The fresh mount that Brown received came by way of the Reverend Jonas Clarke. It was Clarke's own horse, well saddled and well bridled, and Clarke was happy to lend it. The reverend suspected, as he would say, that the British soldiers "were out upon some evil design."

Two others of the Lexington resistance—Nathan Munroe, second cousin to William, and Benjamin Tidd, thirty-two years old—also set off on horses, heading the four and a half miles north toward Bedford, to tell the Patriots there about the British soldiers who were out riding in the county. Sanderson, Loring, and Brown had the far trickier assignment. They would be trailing, and hoping to stake out, nine armed and experienced men. "We agreed if we found the officers, we would return to give information," Sanderson said.

So the three men rode away from Buckman Tavern and out into the Middlesex night, following the road to where they believed the British Regulars had gone. These Patriot riders—and the other two men, riding north—still knew little of what was imminent. They didn't know what was already happening that night, nor did they understand what would soon unfold.

Revere never knew what sort of horse he might get, what temperament it might have. Would it shy when he came near? Might it rear or nicker or flinch? The horse that Revere now received did none of those things. She belonged to Samuel Larkin, an elder of Charlestown, and she came to Revere by way of Larkin's son, John, the deacon of the First Congregational Church. He lived just off the main square. The mare was led out and she stood, stamping gently. The Larkins had named her Brown Beauty. "A very good horse," Revere would say. Revere put his hand on Brown Beauty's flank and spoke calmly into her ear, and then he looked out over the water he'd just crossed, at sloops floating there and at the shape of the HMS *Somerset* rising far above the surface. He'd made it cleanly past the great warship, and the next part of the journey was upon him.

Revere held the reins with one hand, then reached forward and took hold of the cantle with the other. He put his left boot into the stirrup and swung his right leg up over the mare's back. Revere could feel the heat and the flesh of the horse against his thighs and calves. He checked the bridle—the curb chain and the throatlatch. He made sure the girth was properly tightened. It could be easy at times like this, when every minute seems to matter, to neglect the small details, to hurry through or to fall into the eager rider's trap: *I'll fix it on the way.* Tonight was too important to cut corners or take a needless risk. Every detail needed to be in order.

Revere gripped the reins and assembled himself on the flat saddle and took in that first feeling of being up on the horse. The mare, Brown Beauty, snorted gently and champed, feeling the new weight and new balance of the rider on her back. Revere, fixing now his hold on the reins and quickly flattening back his shoulders, touched the horse on her long neck and then at her withers, readying her and himself: the moment before.

Revere sat the horse and began to ride, away from the center of Charlestown and out onto the long, muddied road that ran from the river to Lexington and then to Concord, the road the British soldiers were on. He rode with a sense of moment and enterprise, certain and clear, knowing the battle was at hand.

This was the battle the Patriots had so long imagined

and thought through and discussed, their conviction overcoming their dread. Revere could remember how the Masons had been at the Green Dragon Tavern that December night in 1773, a gathering to celebrate the feast of St. John the Evangelist less than two weeks after so many of those same Patriots had thrown the tea into Boston Harbor. Dozens of men came to the tavern for that feast, a catholic assemblage sworn to secrecy and to one another. With the Tea Party done, they now understood that they were capable of such audacious resistance, that this was the sort of thing they could do again. The men at the tavern knew as they spoke to one another that night that they were each willing to take a risk that might unravel their lives. Revere could remember other times at the Green Dragon and talking with Joseph Warren in the upper rooms about the things that Warren saw and believed. And how Warren could use his words to rouse and inspire! Always Revere had been able, as surely and capably as any person in the movement, to put those words into action. As he came away from Charlestown, the moon was higher now, gibbous and white and bright.

He took the mare quickly to an ambling gait, then spurred her faster still. Here, close by the town, Revere had no need to pause or sound the alarm. People had seen the lanterns, and Richard Devens and John Larkin and Colonel William Conant and the others would make it known that the Regulars were out. The mare ran easily beneath

Revere, her head high, her tail out behind her. They must have covered the mile to the edge of town, to Charlestown Neck, in three minutes or less.

And where now was William Dawes? Had he made it, shuffling along in his clever, drunken-bumpkin charade, past the guards at Boston Neck? Had he found a horse in Roxbury and struck out toward Lexington? Or had the redcoats taken Dawes in, sent him back into Boston, or held him at the guardhouse?

Revere rode on, over and past Charlestown Neck, Brown Beauty in her full four-beat gait, smooth over the flat road and smooth when the road rose and fell. The light was at their back and the after-rain air held the scent of spring. "Very pleasant," as Revere would describe it. He kept the horse moving at a high pace and then, another half mile on, Revere in the shadowy light saw movement ahead of him, beneath the boughs of a tree at a narrow part of the road. Two men on horseback. He pulled up the horse and came to a stop, "nearly opposite," he would recall, "where Mark was hung in chains."

Mark had been an enslaved man who, in 1755 at the age of thirty, was convicted of poisoning his enslaver. Mark was put to the gallows and his body then gibbeted and left in that public space next to the road outside Charlestown, to decompose and to be seen by all who passed. By 1775 he would have been skull and bones. Gibbeting was not entirely uncommon in Massachusetts Bay during the 1750s, though it was primarily the gibbeting of pirates and criminal sailors, who were left to hang on the islands of Boston Harbor, a rougher seafarers' milieu. Someone hung in chains in so conspicuous and traveled a spot as the road near Charlestown Neck, a place families might pass on the way to market or meetinghouse, was more a vestige of the England left behind. The hard sight of Mark became a known landmark—Revere cited it twenty-three years after the ride, aware that the reference would be understood. Over time and as more was learned, Mark hung in chains could come to serve as a haunting reminder not so much of what he had finally done, but of what had been done to him.

THE

Last & Dying Words of

M A R K, Aged about 30 Years,

A Negro Man who belonged to the late Captain *John Codman*, of *Charlestown*;

Who was executed at *Cambridge*, the 18th of *September*, 1755, for Poysoning his abovesaid Master; is as follows, *viz.*

AS I am condemn'd to die by the just Law of GOD and Man for the heinous Sin of Murther, so I would give Glory to GOD in confessing many of my innumerable Crimes, whereby I have justly incur'd the highest Displeasure of the omnipotent Being, who in Anger has left me to the perpetrating such Crimes as to bring me to this shameful, awful Punishment, which may be a dreadful Warning to the Pursuers of my crimson Crimes, and by the Blessing of GOD may prove beneficial to all my Fellow Mortals.

I WAS Born in *Barbados* sometime in the Year 1725, in a reputable Family, and leaving my native Place very Young, came to *Boston*, where Mr. *Henry Caswell* bought me, with whom I tarried some Time, and then was sold to Mr. *Salter*, the Brazier, who learn'd me to read, and educated me as tenderly as one of his own Children. Then I was sold to Mr. *Joseph Thomas* of *Plimouth*, who treated me with the same Kindness that Mr. *Salter* did. Then Mr. *John Codman* of *Charlestown* bought me, with whom I continued till my fatal Delusion, by two Negro Women, *Phillis* and *Phebe*, my Fellow Servants, who wickedly enticed me to procure them Poyson to destroy my Master; for which Crime I am heartily sorry, and would fly to the Blood of *Jesus Christ*, which is able to wash me from the Impurity and Pollution of my innumerable Crimes, and cleanse me from the Blood of my poor Master, which I unjustly and wilfully shed; and am heartily sorry not only for thus destroying my Master, but for breaking up his Family, and leaving so many innocent Children Orphans.

My Master let me live in *Boston* with my Wife, and go out to work. I have most grievously provoked the great GOD to Anger, by repeatedly breaking his holy Day, in going out of his House and resorting to private Places with my wicked Companions in drinking and Carousing on that holy Day, a Time that I should have improv'd in Meditation and Prayer. I have most sinfully abus'd and misimprov'd his manifold Favours to my fatal Disadvantage, and have wilfully neglected to work out my Salvation; all which Sins GOD has call'd into Remembrance, and has justly left me to the perpetrating this horrid Crime.

I was entic'd by those two Negro Women to procure them Poyson, and being left of God at that Time, for my former Iniquities, I went to Dr. *Clarke's* Negro Fellow, *Robbin*, and entic'd him to get me some Poyson, to whom I told horrid Lies before I could get it of him, which could be no other than the Work of the Devil. I told him I wanted it to kill three Pigs, and he being wholly ignorant of my bloody Design, gave it me accordingly.

As to the being accessary to the Death of any other besides my poor Master, I absolutely deny, nor did I ever hear of it till I was confin'd in Prison.

As to the Crime for which I am to die, i.e. of destroying my Master in procuring Poyson for the Negro Women, is as follows:

The two Negro Women, my Fellow Servants (one of which suffers Death with me) enticed me to get the Poyson for them, for which horrible Fact we both deserve Death; it has been conniving this two Years by those two Negro Women *Phillis* and *Phebe*. *Phebe* confess'd to me she had been giving it to my Master these two Years past at different Times.

After I was detected and put in Goal, *Phebe* (She was an Evidence in Behalf of the King;) intended to poison me, that I might not bring both out; but I had taken it from her and hid it amongst the Coal behind the Bellows in my Master's Blacksmith's Shop; and when I had been in Goal about four Days I confess'd where I had put said Poyson, and Mr. *Kettle* went and found it in the Place where I said it was. *Phebe* came to the Prison Grates to desire me not to confess any Thing for they could not hurt me. The Day I was committed, I call'd my Fellow-Servant *Pompey* to shew him the Vial of Poyson which I had taken from *Phillis*, which *Phebe* let her have to hide, but the Officer took me before I had an Opportunity of letting *Pompey* see it. *Phebe* the Day before my Master died, danc'd about in the abovementioned Blacksmith's Shop, mocking my Master when in the bitter Pangs of Death, and came to me after that on the Wharff, while I was in the Necessary House; and I asked her how my Master did? she made answer, the *Old Dog* was just gone, and she would stick as close to him as his Shirt to his Back, and not only so, but she would cut down the *Old Tree*, and then would lop off the Branches.—— *Phebe* had Poyson in the House long before I procur'd her any, and us'd to give my Master Copperas which caus'd a wracking Pain in his Belly, which I thought very Cruel, seeing Master treated her better than any of us Servants. The Night before my Master died, she watched with him, who was in great Misery until the Time of his Death.—Next Morning after watching with my Master, she went up to his Chamber to see him, and he ask'd her how she did after Watching, she told him she was very well, and wish'd he was as well as she was.——My two young Mistress's being then present, who put so much Confidence in her as to trust her with the Teas my Master drank; little thinking of her fatal Design against him.— Some Time before this, she told her Husband, (*Quaco*) when at *Charlestown* to see her, to desire me to get some more of that Trade, for it was a good Opportunity now her Master was already Sick, which I accordingly got twice for her from Dr. *Gibbins's* Negro, *Carr*; and to my certain Knowledge went unto her self to this Negro to get more, but he had not an Opportunity then to get any; so she sent me to him another Time for it, and he (the said *Carr*) told me he would send her none, because *Phebe* had told him she had a Design to Poyson somebody in the House; and he told me, he'd ask her Husband (*Quaco*) first, whether he was willing, and then pretended to me that he was angry with her; (though I believe he was as knowing in the Affair as I was;) for he was contriving all he could to get her over to *Boston* to live with him, and said, he would not value *Forty Pounds* if he could do it.——

Now concerning the burning of my Master's Shop, I can declare I was sick in Bed, which *Phillis* can witness to; Notwithstanding People thinking hard of me, when the Fire was raging I got out of my Bed, though sick and weak, and saved my Master several Pair of Wheels, and let out two Horses which would have been burnt, and at the same Time had like to have lost my own Life in the Attempt. *Phebe* first prepar'd a Chaffin Dish of Coals in the Dwelling-House Cellar, and call'd *Phillis* to set the Shop on Fire.——I observ'd in *Phebe's* Countenance at the Time of the Fire, she looked Guilty, and upon asking her about it, she confess'd that she had prepar'd the Coals for *Phillis* to burn the Shop.

Phebe that Night, in the midst of the Hurry and Confusion, while the Shop was burning, wickedly stole some of the Cloaths thrown out of the Window to be sav'd; which *Phillis* told me of, and to my certain Knowledge, she was a great Thief: She stole Money from my Master, in which I brought her out; and since that, *Phillis* and she stole *One Hundred Pounds* in Money, Part of which I believe to be in *Phebe's* Sister's Hands; the Truth of which *Phillis* has declar'd to me in our Confinement.

Thus I have given you a true, but awful Account of mine and my Accomplices wicked Proceedings: I have justly provok'd GOD to leave me to myself!— My heinous Sins of Sabbath-breaking, Lying, Drinking, Uncleanness, Eye-Service, Neglect of secret and publick Prayer, and the shedding of innocent Blood, loudly call for divine Vengeance. I now sadly experience what a dreadful Thing it is to fall into the Hands of the living GOD— Tho' I am a great Sinner, yet I despair not of the unmerited Mercy of GOD, through JESUS CHRIST; tho' my Sins exceed the Hairs of my Head in Number, and all of a crimson and a Scarlet Dye; yet I hope to find Mercy with that GOD, whose Mercies and Loving-Kindnesses exceed my Sins in Number— Let me beseech you all, my Fellow-Servants, (especially the Women) to take Warning by me, and shun those Vices which have prov'd my Ruin; and which have most grievously provoked a holy God.— I once pursu'd a Course of Vice and Wickedness with some of you, and have been guilty of notorious Crimes; But God has singled me out from amongst you all, that I might not only be a Monument of awful Justice, but hope of his saving Mercy too.

I freely forgive all my Enemies, and fly to JESUS CHRIST, who is willing to save undone Sinners. I heartily thank all the godly Ministers that have visited me while under Confinement, in order to direct me in the Way to eternal Life and Happiness; and can now, Thanks be to GOD, undauntedly look Death in the Face.

GOD be merciful to me a great Sinner. *Amen.*

Mark.

We the Subscribers were present, when Mark acknowledged this to be his last and dying Words.

Isaac Bradish,
James Boyd,
David Cutter,
Samuel Hide.

Sold next to the Prison in Queen-Street.

Account sold near the prison on Queen Street, 1755

12

MARK IN CHAINS

What ran through Revere's mind then, during his momentary pause? Did Revere think—if not in the moment, then later, in his recountings—of the enslaved men and women who were among the citizenry of Boston, those who came to market to barter and shop on an enslaver's behalf? Did he, in alluding to this memory of that spectral shape of Mark in chains, think of the child Nulgar, whom his maternal grandmother had once enslaved? Upon her death she bequeathed a claim to Nulgar to her son, Thomas, Revere's uncle. Revere never enslaved anyone, nor did he ever live with anyone enslaved. Neither did the high majority of people in Revere's circles. But some did. The presence and practice of enslavement was part of Revere's world.

Earlier that same night, when Revere had gone to Joseph Warren's house, who had opened the great front door to let him in? Was it Dr. Warren himself? His apprentice, Eustis? Or might it have been the young man Warren had purchased in 1770? Warren had made that agreement with Joshua Green, from whom Warren rented the house on Hannover Street. Green's widowed mother, Elizabeth, and the enslaved young man remained living in the house after Warren moved in.

The bill of sale had the dateline Boston, June 28, 1770. It read in Warren's handwriting:

> *I the Subscriber having this day purchas'd a Negro Boy of Joshua Green have made the following conditions with him: That I will add Ten Pounds of Lawfull Money to be paid in Potter's Ware manufactur'd in this Town in three years to the Thirty pounds first agreed for if in 3 Months from this date I shall think the negro worth the money & if I do not think him worth the additional ten pounds I will reconvey him to said Green with he returning the two Notes I gave him for the negro, one for £17 and one for £13, both of them bearing date herewith.*
>
> *Joseph Warren*

Later in the document Warren agreed that in the event he should die, "the within mentioned negro shall become the property" of Green.

It was Joseph Warren who would in 1772 deploy the metaphor of slavery in his oration at the site of the 1770 Boston Massacre. For the colonists to accept the Crown's attempt at unilaterally imposed taxation would be to "admit at once that we are slaves and have no property of our own," Warren said. And it was Warren who would write so defiantly in the Suffolk Resolves, paragraph four, that the Townshend Acts the Crown sought to impose on the colonists should be rejected "as the attempts of a wicked administration to enslave America."

And yet in 1770 Warren had agreed to "purchase" a human being, with the intent to control him. And then Warren would determine whether that human being was "worth the money" or should be returned. What was it that allowed for this contradiction, this hypocrisy of thought and action? As a doctor, Warren treated and nurtured men and women of any race and any descent. He was known for that.

Enslavement touched the lives of others in the Patriot leadership. John Hancock lived among enslaved servants as a child and may have inherited those enslaved people upon his uncle's death. It is not believed that Hancock ever bought or sold a slave. Samuel Adams's wife, Elizabeth, was once given an enslaved woman; Samuel insisted that the woman be freed. In 1752 Ruth Buckman, who would run the Buckman Tavern with her husband, John, sold an enslaved person to a prominent Lexington man named William Reed. John Sullivan, the resistance leader with whom Revere conjoined on his critical mission to Portsmouth, New Hampshire, in December of 1774, had rooms at the back of his house where his enslaved servants lived.

Some sixteen thousand African American people lived in New England in 1775, including about fifty-two hundred in Massachusetts—somewhere around 1.5 percent of the colony's overall population. Many of those people were free and many were not. Two decades earlier, in 1754, there were believed to be twenty-seven hundred enslaved people in Massachusetts. By the eve of the Revolution that number had lessened considerably. Enslavement then was not anything close to prevalent. Neither was it rare.

Enslaved African Americans were first brought to Boston by ship in the late 1630s. As the 1700s dawned and proceeded, advertisements to buy, sell, or trade enslaved men, women, and children regularly appeared in the *Boston Gazette* and the *Boston News-Letter*. The enslaved population in New England, as well as the number of enslavers, grew steadily over those years. Enslaved people were listed in wills and other legal documents as chattel alongside other assets. In 1718 an inventory of property described by a Roxbury estate holder, Thomas Mory, read in part, "Horse and Oxen 3 Cows 1 Bull 2 Heifers a Yearling A Negro Boy 2 pairs of Loons and 3 Swine."

Most typically in Massachusetts enslaved people worked as house servants. Children could be taken from their mothers and sold. Most married couples—among them Mark and his wife—were separated and might be bound to different enslavers. Few enslaved families remained intact.

In the 1760s and early 1770s, as the ideas that led to the American Revolution formed and were articulated, and as sentiment grew that the colonies needed to slip the yokes of imperial rule, so did sentiment turn more sharply toward the abolishment of slavery. Some critical Patriots could not abide the discrepancy in a movement for freedom that did not apply to all. "I have, through my whole life held the practice of slavery in such abhorrence," John Adams would write in 1795. "Though I have lived for many years in times when the practice was not disgraceful; when the best men in my vicinity thought it not inconsistent with their character."

In 1764 James Otis, the brilliant and enormously influential Patriot leader and lawyer whose views and rhetorical style helped ignite the Revolutionary fire, published a pamphlet, *The Rights of the British Colonies Asserted and Proved.* The document suggested that humans had natural, God-given rights, and it loudly articulated a resistance to being taxed by the Crown. "The colonists are by the law of nature freeborn, as indeed all men are, white or black," Otis wrote. He was a mentor to both Samuel and John Adams. "Slavery is so vile and miserable an estate of man, and so directly opposite to the generous temper and courage of our nation," Otis wrote. He added that it was "a clear truth that those who every day barter away other men's liberty, will soon care little for their own."

In the decade following Otis's treatise and leading up to the Revolution, more than a dozen enslaved people brought legal action seeking freedom from their enslavers. Some were successful. Many of the enslaved men and women of Massachusetts were literate and educated and were aware of the prevailing intellectual winds.

It may be that Joseph Warren, clearly attuned to this evolving landscape and perhaps lately enlightened—his parents were enslavers, his descendants abolitionists—had freed the enslaved young man he had purchased from Joshua Green. After Warren was killed at Bunker Hill in June of 1775, there was no mention of the enslaved man in Warren's will.

When Revere alerted the Minutemen and the townspeople across Middlesex County on the night of April 18, African American men were among those who responded. They would join at Lexington and join at Concord. Peter Salem from Framingham and Cuff Whittemore from Cambridge and other men, from Stoneham and Braintree and Brookline. They were willing to die in defense of a budding nation's principles, just as the white resistance fighters were. Peter Salem would, at the Battle of Bunker Hill, have a hand in killing Major John Pitcairn of the Royal Army.

In 1780, the Massachusetts Constitution declared that "all men are born free and equal and have . . . the right of enjoying and defending their lives and liberties." Over the next years a series of court cases pushed that implication into law, making enslavement illegal in the colony. The 1790 census for Massachusetts put the number of enslaved people in the colony at zero.

Mark committed his murder and was put to death in a time just before the developments that led to the push toward the end of enslavement in Massachusetts. Mark's story and his displayed remains may have provided additional impetus for abolitionists, working as a reminder—a detour off the dirt road near Charlestown Neck, into the swamp of America's collective sin. The dramatic public executions of Mark and Phillis—an enslaved woman who was Mark's accomplice—occurred in Cambridge when Revere was twenty years old. Such executions made news. Revere would have known about it. Here is a newspaper account, dated September 11, 1755:

> Last Tuesday in the Afternoon, at the Affixes held at Cambridge, in the Country of Middlesex, Phillis,

> a Negro Woman and Mark, a Negro Man, Servants to the late Capt. Codman of Charles-Town, deceased, who were found Guilty of poisoning their Master, received Sentence of Death.
>
> The Said Phillis, to be drawn to the Place of Execution, and there burnt to Death; and the said Mark, to be drawn to the Place of Execution, and there to be hang'd by the Neck till he be dead:— Which sentences are to be ordered to be put in Execution upon Thursday the 18th Day of September.

MARK WAS HANGED in Cambridge, in the middle of the afternoon, before a crowd described in the *Boston Gazette* as "the Greatest Number of Spectators ever known on Such an Occasion." Phillis, as the *Evening-Post* related, was "burned at a stake about ten yards distant from the gallows." Both had been convicted of murder and—because they had killed their enslaver—of treason. There in the public square, by the prison on Queen Street, Mark delivered a thoughtful, often eloquent speech. He admitted to poisoning John Codman, expressed remorse before Jesus Christ, and outlined some of the circumstances of his life. "God be merciful to me, a great sinner. Amen" were his final words.

Mark was born into enslavement in Barbados in 1725.

His parents or his grandparents had been taken from Africa. When Mark was, as he recalled, "very young," he was brought to Boston and sold. Over the years he had a series of three enslavers before being bought by John Codman of Charlestown. Codman had sailed as a captain at sea and now worked as a saddler and general merchant. He kept at least two enslaved women, Phillis and Phoebe, to serve him at his home and workplace in Charlestown. Mark also worked and served at times in Charlestown, but he lived primarily in Boston, where he worked various jobs for various people, then handed a portion of what he earned to Codman. While in Boston, Mark got married and had a child.

Years before the fatal poisoning, seeking to disrupt Codman's financial stability in hopes that he would have to sell them, Mark, Phillis, and Phoebe teamed up to burn down Codman's workshop. "I threw a coal of fire into some shavings between the blacksmith's shop and the workhouse," Phillis recalled during her murder trial. Mark had given instructions and had put the wood shavings in place. The workshop burned to the ground, but Codman weathered the loss. He did not sell any of the enslaved people nor, at that time, did he suspect them of the arson.

Codman could get violent. He once badly beat another of his enslaved men, Tom, inflicting permanent damage to one of Tom's eyes. After Codman was stricken by the poison but before it was clear that he would die, Tom, according to Mark's testimony, said that he hoped Codman would "never get up again for his eye's sake." There was also reason to suspect that Codman, a widower, was sexually assaulting Phoebe—raping her. After the poisoning, Phoebe was sold off out of New England and did not testify about any of the crimes.

Not long before the murder, Codman had ordered Mark to come back to Charlestown from Boston, taking him away from his wife and child. "What reason did Mark give for poisoning his master?" Phillis was asked during her trial. "He said he was uneasy and wanted to have another master, and he was concerned for Phoebe and I, too," she replied. Phillis also testified that Mark had read the Bible and determined that "it was no sin to kill him if they did not lay violent hands on him so as to shed blood."

Mark obtained poison—both arsenic and black lead—from an African American man named Robin, who was enslaved near Clark's Wharf and thus near the house where Paul Revere grew up. As a child Revere, garrulous and social across all classes, may well have known Robin, at least incidentally, from around the wharf.

Poisoning Codman proved neither simple nor immediate. Over several days Phillis and Phoebe, at Mark's direction, put poison in Codman's "chocolate," in his porridge, and finally in his "water gruel," before the arsenic finally took hold and had the desired effect. The coroner's inquest determined that "John Codman came to his death by poison procured by his negro man Mark." The witnesses who sealed the inquest with their oaths included three men of Charlestown, Richard Devens, John Larkin, and Samuel Larkin, all of whom became coincidentally prominent in Paul Revere's ride.

Twenty years after Mark's execution, his remains hung in their perpetual night encampment on the northern side of the road to Charlestown, just near the point where Revere stopped on the night of April 18. Soon after that night, as the American Revolution grew in scope and then got fully underway, Mark's skeleton was removed from its chains and taken down.

John Hancock's trunk

13

THE RIDE

REVERE PULLED GENTLY ON THE REINS, SLOWING the powerful mare and continuing at an easier pace along the road toward the two men on horseback beneath the trees. The men were on Revere's left, on the southern side of the road, holding still in their saddles. The body of Mark hung on the northern side of the road, and the moon was risen at Revere's back. Revere's frock coat and waistcoat were made of wool. The air felt cooler now away from the city. He advanced still closer to the men. "I discovered they were British officers," Revere would say. "I got near enough to see their holsters and cockades."

Suddenly the officers broke into action. "One of them started his horse towards me and the other up the road—I supposed to get ahead of me," Revere said. Revere did not hesitate. He knew the roads into and out of Charlestown, knew there was an alternate way to Lexington. He and the two British Regulars were half a mile past where the road had forked behind him, where he had broken left to take the more direct route west. "I turned my horse very quick," Revere said.

He rode straight back the way he'd come, Brown Beauty quick to full speed on the sodden earth. The charging officer followed in close pursuit. For two hundred yards, for three hundred, the officer bore in, plenty near enough to fire his pistol at Revere had he chosen to do so. Then he tried to make a move. "Endeavoring to cut me off," Revere would recall, the officer "got into a clay pond," stopping his progress just like that. "I got clear of him," Revere said.

He left the Regulars behind and rode hard back to the fork near Charleston Neck and turned Brown Beauty "upon full gallop for Mistick Road"—a northerly swing that would add some wending distance to Revere's ride but would also, in a benefit, allow him to spread the alarm wider still. He rode for three miles or more through woods and open farmland, still at Brown Beauty's high pace, and then clattered over the wooden bridge that crossed the

Mystic River. On the far bank, in Medford, said Revere, "I awaked the captain of the Minutemen."

WHAT ENABLED PAUL Revere to ride so well and deftly that night, to meet the moment that had such weight upon it, to remain unruffled, to improvise and deliver? There might have been any opportunity—most particularly when the Regulars interceded so intensely—to lose his focus, to get ruinously waylaid, to wind up in a clay pond himself. Revere was a great express rider, the best the Patriots ever had. And yet riding on the back of an unfamiliar horse, believing that the fate of the resistance depended on the outcome, knowing that his own reputation might be defined by how this ride, this venture, turned out—all that might have been enough to cause even the most talented express rider to falter. Revere thrived.

"People choke under pressure because they worry," wrote the cognitive scientist Sian Beilock in her field-defining book, *Choke: What the Secrets of the Brain Reveal About Getting It Right When You Have To*. "They worry about the situation, its consequences, and what others will think. They worry about what they will lose if they fail to succeed." In short, those who struggle may be overthinking things—Hamlet dithering, Vizzini in a battle of wits, Greg Norman on the greens at Augusta.

Revere was none of those. "Cool in thought, ardent

in action," his obituary read. Over the sweep of his long life, Revere *acted*—in his immediate responses and in his resourceful approach to life and work. He'd forge a warped plate into a silver bowl on a dying flame. A self-made silversmith, he became a self-taught engraver and a self-taught dentist and then a man who would teach himself to roll copper and to cast bells. Times changed and Revere changed with them.

On the night of April 18, 1775, Revere, three months and three weeks past his fortieth birthday, was imbued with the crucial background to help him perform at his best. If you're used to operating under pressure, even to a lesser degree, you're less likely to rattle when the pressure builds. Revere had ridden in high haste to Philadelphia to deliver the Suffolk Resolves. He had ridden to Portsmouth to rally the militia. He'd carried out more than a dozen rides for the movement, and invariably he had faced the threat or at least the specter of capture close at hand. Revere was among the threescore Patriots whose name appeared on the Crown's expressed list of "enemies." There was heat on Revere and he could stand that heat.

Innumerable hours of behavioral and cognitive research have been spent trying to understand how professional people—academics, politicians, lawyers, doctors, and most conspicuously athletes—can be best suited and best prepared to perform optimally under pressure.

Beilock's seminal book considers people across the landscape of endeavors, and in the later pages she posits eight key rules for helping the skilled performer succeed when the time arrives. Two of those rules have no verifiable relevance to Revere's ride: find a mantra to say to yourself, and make a slight change in your technique. The other six rules, though, might have been drawn from the short list of Paul Revere's personal characteristics. They might serve as a retrofitted blueprint for the ride:

◊ Distract yourself (Revere clearly did, noting his surroundings and the atmosphere of the night)
◊ Don't slow down (Revere: "I turned my horse very quick")
◊ Practice under stress (as mentioned)
◊ Don't dwell (Revere did not)
◊ Focus on the outcome, not the mechanics (Revere was bound for Lexington, no matter what obstacles he encountered)
◊ Focus on the positive (as the hale Revere did, resolutely)

There's an additional, more specific, way to increase your chances for success, Beilock writes: "Pausing to assess the situation." We can see Revere standing there off the shore in Charlestown that night as Brown Beauty was being prepared. We can see him under the big refulgent moon, considering the river passage behind him, envisioning the road ahead, feeling ready for whatever might lie in store.

THE CAPTAIN OF the Medford Minutemen, Isaac Hall, was thirty-six years old and had lived in Medford all his life. He owned a distillery in partnership with his brother. Isaac and his wife, Abigail, had a ten-year-old daughter and a six-year-old son, and the family lived in a three-story house that rose up off the northern side of the road not far from the banks of the Mystic River, a square bulk of black shadow against the silvered sky. A loyalist owned the land that abutted the eastern edge of Hall's land, and a doctor owned land on another side. Revere stopped at the house and roused Hall, telling him that the Regulars had come out in a force of hundreds—grenadiers and light infantry crossing the Charles River—and were bound for Lexington. At Revere's first words Hall knew that it was time to gather and rally the men.

And then Revere left Isaac Hall and continued on. At the Medford Square he met a mounted Patriot, Martin Herrick, a doctor, age twenty-seven, and Revere told Herrick of the Regulars advancing. Herrick, who was neither part of the Committee of Correspondence nor had any defined role in the militia, and who would not be suspect for traveling at night—to appearances he was simply a doctor out on an emergency round—knew the name and standing of Paul Revere. Herrick took the news back to where he lived, riding northward, away from the road and side roads where the British patrol might have been, to the vaster farmland of Lynnfield and to the town of Reading, stopping at the tavern to spread the news, then bringing word to another doctor he knew, the young captain of the Reading Minutemen, John Brooks. So that now, as the night deepened, the men in those more northern towns, Lynn and Lynnfield and Reading, were assembling and soon setting off toward Lexington on horseback, their fowling pieces locked and belted to their sides, fixing to meet the Regulars where they were.

Revere rode on along High Street, passing the old school and then, a quarter mile beyond the house of Isaac Hall, passing the wide, newly built Medford Meeting House. High Street began to slope upward, and the terrain became stonier around the sides of the road as Revere and Brown Beauty climbed, ascending Rock Hill. The Mystic River lay below them, to their left.

The road descended off the rise and came into flatland, fenced and tended, and Revere followed the road as it neared and then veered farther away from the Mystic River, the earth wet and sometimes sodden beneath Brown Beauty's hooves. Along the way small pools of water pocked the road and mud splattered up from Brown Beauty's forelegs against her sides and against Revere's boots and buckskin pants.

Revere rode on and again crossed over the Mystic River by bridge. High Street became Medford Street, and Revere rode into the town of Menotomy, past where the meetinghouse stood and the Russell Store, and then beyond that Cutler's Tavern and the wooden houses set just back into the fields. Here the road was known to those who lived alongside it as the Concord Road.

Revere was now more than three miles, closer to four, from where he had left Isaac Hall and then Martin Herrick in Medford. All through those miles Revere spread word of the Regulars' advance. He passed the homes of Gibson and Swan and Caldwell and Smith and Johnson and Cutter and Hill—such names and many others that he would never reveal, would always keep protected. In remembrance of the night Revere would say simply, "I alarmed almost every house till I got to Lexington."

There may have been eight hundred people living in Medford then, or nine hundred, and maybe as many in Menotomy. Delivering the alarm did not in each case take much time, didn't much slow Revere on his intended path. He spoke directly and firmly, and his words came as tinder to a wanting flame. The Patriots he met were ready to act. "We are determined in a firm, virtuous, manly and joint way," the leaders of Chelmsford had resolved in the months before Revere's ride, "to secure and defend our liberties, those liberties purchased for us by our ancestors, at the expense of so much blood and treasure. Before they are wrenched from us we will struggle hard, very hard for them, considering ourselves as the guardians of unborn millions. . . . In freedom we're born and in freedom we'll die."

In Chelmsford, twenty miles northwest of Medford, a messenger would arrive with news of the British mission, and there would be no hesitation. The militia captains fired their alarm guns and beat the drums to rouse every Chelmsford Minuteman from his home or farm. And when they gathered as planned at the rock near the heart of town, the local parson, Parson Bridge, suggested they leave off their horses for a short while and go into the meetinghouse for prayer. But the militia leader, Captain John Ford, defied Parson Bridge—they had no time for prayer! he said—and the Minutemen, dozens of them, rode from Chelmsford down the southern route to Lexington and Concord.

With Revere their progenitor, mounted messengers would over the next hours course across Middlesex County and into Essex County and Norfolk County, into the counties of Bristol and Worcester. All that night and into the day they would ride to rally the locals throughout

Massachusetts Bay and would soon after ride farther still, heading south and north into the neighboring colonies so that all might know that the time had arrived.

They fanned out that night and early morning. Some messengers had been alerted by Revere and others had been alerted by somcone who had in their turn been alerted by Revere. Some messengers had heard about the lanterns shown in the Old North Church. They rode short essays and longer journeys. They took the regular roads, galloped through open fields, crossed river bridges, and found wooded paths. They stopped once or twice or several times to give the news.

Even then many of the riders were shrouded in mystery and concealment, few of them wanting their names to be known, to be attached to a treason they could be hanged for. That night and over the days to come, reports would rise of a shadowy horseman crossing a bridge or of an unnamed voice calling out the alarm as he rode past. Here people spoke of seeing a rider without a hat, there of meeting a rider on a tall white horse.

There were the stories, in the time that soon followed, of Israel Bissell, a twenty-three-year-old postrider. At the bidding of a Committee of Safety leader—fifty-nine-year-old militia colonel Joseph Palmer—Bissel set out during the day of April 19 riding the Post Road south to tell of how the Regulars had come to Lexington and blood had been shed. Bissell left from Watertown, just west of Cambridge, charged by Palmer to "alarm the country quite to Connecticut." Soon after, word spread that Bissell had in fact traveled well past Connecticut, all the way down to Philadelphia, a five-day journey covering close to 350 miles, alerting the towns and countryside, declaring, "The war has begun!" He drew notice wherever he came through. To the locals he was sometimes nameless or was sometimes, in the messages that passed from place to place, called Trail or Train or Isaac.

But was Israel Bissell in fact Isaac Bissell, a different postrider who lived in Suffield, Connecticut? Isaac Bissell would later receive payment from the Massachusetts House of Representatives for riding express in April of 1775. Or was the mounted messenger rather Israel Bissell, Sr., father to the Watertown postrider? And how many mounts did Bissell—whether Trail or Train or Isaac or Israel—take along this journey? "All persons are desired to furnish him with fresh horses, as they may be needed," Palmer had written in a note that Bissell carried.

Did Bissell deliver a message in the farmlands of northern Connecticut on one day, then ride into New Haven, seventy-five miles south, the next? Was Bissell in truth more than one rider? Were there several messengers who completed, in relay style, the long route to Philadelphia?

These were the kinds of tales and conjectures that would unfold in the kitchens and taverns and meetinghouses. The embellishments of myth and uncertain detail attached to the firm bones of fact, to the rides of Paul Revere and William Dawes and the others who left their imprint and their touch on history in those extraordinary, nation-shaping hours.

That night at 2:00 A.M., so now April 19, 1775, a messenger arrived in Tewksbury, just east of Chelmsford, and told John Trull, the Minuteman captain who lived near the southern bank of the Merrimack River, "The British are on their way to Concord and I have alerted all the towns from Charlestown to here!" Captain Trull from his bedroom window fired three gunshots, the agreed-upon alarm, and the sound went across the Merrimack River into the town of Dracut, and in this way the Minutemen there were warned. Soon those men from Tewksbury and Dracut, their horses tacked, rode off and into the fight.

In Woburn, where the local ranks of Minutemen had only lately been formed, a messenger arrived in the last darkness before sunrise, not shouting but knocking on doors to tell that the battle was nearly upon them in Lexington, five miles to the west.

The alarm came by messenger to Andover, to Billerica and to Bedford, where Benjamin Tidd and Nathan Munroe had a few hours earlier arrived from Buckman Tavern with news of the nine British officers riding through the county. When the Bedford Minutemen learned the larger truth—of the great column of redcoats on the march—they met at the Fitch Tavern in the early morning. Militia captain Jonathan Wilson, who would die on the battlefield that same day, said to the gathering, "It is a cold breakfast, boys, but we will give the British a hot dinner. We'll have every dog of them before night."

In Acton, six miles west of Concord, the militia leader Francis Faulkner heard his son call out to him through the dark of night, "Father, there's a horse coming on the full run, and he's bringing news!" Faulkner met the horseman and took that news ("Rouse your Minutemen . . . the British are marching!") and fired his gun three times for the town to know. In Pepperell and Littleton, in Newton and Needham, in Danvers and Dedham, messengers arrived, and captains fired their guns and knowledge that the Regulars were out began to spread.

Messengers arrived at houses and farms in the moonlit early-morning hours and in the predawn and as the day began to break. Sometimes one mounted messenger gave way to another, who continued on, and sometimes two horsemen rode in tandem. Some messengers were experienced riders—postriders or express riders or militiamen—but many simply took the assignment impromptu, chosen by random circumstance. Together these riders formed the face and voice of the start of the American Revolution. Organized in a fashion, but loosely so, an outgrowth, in both spirit and practical measure, of the network of express riders devised by Samuel Adams and elevated by Paul Revere. In Worcester, which lay more than forty miles from the Charlestown line, a parched and dusty rider arrived at the square in front of the church, where his horse collapsed in exhaustion.

The messengers reached town after town that night, but they did not reach everywhere. Not every farm and dwelling across those sprawling counties got the news in its early stage. News traveled fast but not always fast enough. The course of the alarm, every rider knew, could die in the emptiness of open land.

And even where the messages were received, would enough of the Minutemen and the militia indeed respond quickly? And would they respond again when the moment to fight came? To feel the force and menace of an enemy? So many of the Patriot militia were young. So many of them were untested by the heat and danger, the din and violence and fear, of the battlefield. Traveling through the countryside delivering the news and then moving on, there was no way for Revere, or any other rider, to know how successful the errand would or would not be.

THERE'S A STORY from the time, told well in the *History of Middlesex County,* a collection of accounts assembled in 1890 by the biographer D. Hamilton Hurd, about the farmer Ephraim Warren. He was plowing his land in Townsend, near the dam, forty miles from Charlestown, thirty miles out from Lexington, when he heard the alarm, given in Townsend through the firing of a town cannon. Warren stopped his work and detached his plow and went to his house and called to his wife, "Mollie, the Regulars are coming, and I am going. Give me my gun." It was morning then in Townsend, the sun well up, and by the time Ephraim Warren learned the greater details of what was happening, and by the time he reached Concord, the conflict there had ended. Warren came upon an empty place with the bodies of the dead on the earth, and the moment past.

And what if too many of the other responders had arrived so late? What if Revere and the messengers whom Revere launched had not delivered the word so quickly? Imagine if Revere had not gotten the lanterns shown in the Old North Church? Or if he had not slipped free from Boston at all that night, not snuck past the HMS *Somerset,* not alerted Richard Devens and the other actors in Charlestown and beyond? What if Revere had strayed from his intensity and his diligence? *I alarmed almost every house till I got to Lexington.* Word of the Regulars' action would eventually have come to the towns, and the militias would have responded, but would they have responded in time? What if so many others had received the later notice as it was received by Ephraim Warren in Townsend?

In the early-morning light of April 19, 1775, the column of British Regulars would be met at the Lexington

Green by scores of Patriot militia. The Regulars moved past them, leaving eight dead in their wake. By the time those redcoats reached Concord, the awaiting Patriots numbered in the hundreds and stood up in some resistance. And then, as the redcoats—with their plans to destroy the Patriot stores in Concord all but blunted—marched back toward Lexington, thousands of Patriot militiamen lined the road. "We were totally surrounded with such incessant fire as it's impossible to conceive," the British lieutenant John Barker would say.

In Lexington, reinforcements arrived for the Regulars, saving them from full surrender. Yet as they continued to march back to Boston, through Menotomy and on to Cambridge, still greater swarms of Patriots covered and blasted their path. "We were fired on by all quarters," Lieutenant Frederick Mackenzie said. The redcoats got back to the Charles River late in the day, having lost many lives, badly wounded and badly beaten. Many of them boarded the HMS *Somerset* for medical care. Those more able returned, chastened, to the Boston camps. The British army would never look at the Patriot resisters the same way again, would never underestimate their ability to fight.

Imagine if on that day, April 19, 1775, the British Regulars had instead pulled off their audacious mission and had their imperial way in Lexington and Concord, had taken what they'd come for and emerged unscathed, or less scathed. Might the Patriots have instead been the chastened ones? Might greater doubt have crept into the American resolve? The Regulars were much better trained and much better funded. How hot would the Patriot fire have remained in the early stages of the Revolution if things had gone the other way at the start? Had Revere not ignited the alarm so powerfully as he did?

EVEN BEFORE THEY encountered the colonists, the redcoats had their troubles that night and early morning—troubles that derived in part from human error and incompetence. The errors, that is, of General Thomas Gage, a leader ambivalent in his taste for war with the Patriots, pushed into action by the Crown, clouded perhaps with the uneasy sense that his wife, Margaret Kemble Gage, opposed the mission and may have hoped to undermine it.

Gage made miscalculations. He didn't think things through. He had some bad luck, though the bad luck proved largely of his own making.

The Regulars, under General Gage's direction, tipped their hand too early, taking the light infantry off its normal duty days before necessary, bringing in the small boats too soon, sending out a patrol so conspicuously on the same day the Royal Army would begin its march. The soldiers crossed the Charles River at too wide a spot and with the current against them. For the crossing Gage had arranged for far too few boats and had designated a problematic landing area. Nor did he come to the shoreline to oversee the operation.

The rowboats that ferried the soldiers were heavily laden with arms, and the river lay shallow near the opposite shore. The redcoats would have to wade to land. "We were wet up to the knees," Lieutenant John Barker recounted. That was not the worst of it. The inlets around the landing area flushed high with tidewater so that even after coming ashore the soldiers would be confronted with marshy terrain and forced to pass, as Barker said, "through a very long ford up to our middies." They were wet and tired and compromised from the start. By the time the Regulars had their boots on solid ground on the road to Lexington, 2:00 A.M. had come and gone. This was more than four hours after Revere left Joseph Warren's house in Boston. And two hours after Revere reached Lexington himself.

Gage had for some time understood the conviction of the Patriots, the strength of their beliefs. "The people are so possessed with the Notions instilled into them, that all Authority is derived from them," he had written to England. And yet as the evening of April 18, 1775, began, it was not hard to imagine that the advantage in the larger fight was to the Crown, to the better-trained, better-equipped British army, and to the general force of human tendency. The Patriots, for all the fervor of their leadership, still had to contend with the daunting power of inertia, of the status quo, of the plain acceptance that so often leads us to bear those ills we have rather than risk the burden of those we don't yet know. The reality of British sovereignty had for generations shaped the lives of Patriots both firm and less committed. It had shaped the lives of just about everyone, either side, who lived on American soil. "We, the heirs and successors of the first planters of this colony, do cheerfully acknowledge George the III to be our rightful sovereign, and that said covenant is the tenure and claim on which are founded our allegiance and submission," wrote Joseph Warren in the 1774 Suffolk Resolves, even while defiantly shucking off the yoke of imperial rule.

That experienced and tested British army would have seemed by most measures to hold the advantage over ordinary Patriots leading happy enough lives. Yet sometime during the overnight of April 18, as Revere rode through the countryside, and the Minutemen saddled up and found their guns, that British advantage was lost.

"But Fortune, O, She is corrupted, changed and won from thee," says Constance to her son, the heir to the throne, in *The Life and Death of King John,* the play that Margaret Kemble Gage called upon to describe the unpredictable heartache and pain of war.

* * *

REVERE RODE OVER the town line into Lexington, moving fast and comfortably on the familiar route. Now there was no stopping. He passed the Munroe Tavern and the Buckman Tavern and the meetinghouse, then arrived at the home of the Reverend Jonas Clarke. Even then William Munroe and the other men who guarded the house did not understand the full seriousness of the night, the size of the British operation, the need to act without delay. They knew only that some British soldiers were riding suspiciously through the area. When, as Munroe would say, "Colonel Paul Revere rode up and requested admittance, I told him that the family had just retired and had requested that they might not be disturbed by any noise about the house."

Responded Revere, in full voice, "Noise? You'll have noise enough before long. The Regulars are coming out."

And then to the left of Revere as he stood talking with Munroe came the sound of a window opening, and John Hancock from his bedroom called out, "Come in, Revere. We're not afraid of you."

It was past midnight now. The main road and the smaller alleys and the homes were all quiet. Aside from some stirring at the Buckman Tavern, few people were about, and the farms were all at rest. Revere wondered at that stillness, the lack of what was known. No British troops had yet molested Lexington—a source of principal relief—but they were assuredly on their way. And no one was aware. "I inquired for Mr. Dawes," Revere would recall. "They said he had not been there."

Revere thought of the two soldiers he had encountered and escaped near Charlestown Neck. He wondered whether Dawes had also been met by a British patrol, and whether that meeting had led to a darker fate. "I supposed that he must have been stopped," Revere would say. "He ought to have been there before me."

AFTER LEAVING JOSEPH Warren's house on Hannover Street some time before Revere arrived, Dawes went to the stables and secured a horse. He tacked the horse, mounted, and then rode through the streets toward Boston Neck, consciously nonchalant in the way that he sat the horse, not wanting to draw attention, nor convey urgency. A cousin of Dawes's followed him on foot, staying well behind but close enough to see whether Dawes would in fact make it past the redcoats manning the Neck.

Dawes jogged slowly on his horse, saddlebags at his sides and a farmer's hat on his head, intending, as one ancestral account put it, "to resemble a countryman on a journey." Dawes approached the guards confidently. He had done this before, on lesser nights. As he drew near, he merged into an easy gait alongside some mounted British soldiers, tavernbound perhaps, men he had come to know and might talk with. In this way Dawes without trouble rode past the guardhouse and out of Boston.

Then Dawes broke from the group of soldiers and trotted off alone, past the George Tavern and past the Roxbury meetinghouse. He turned westward, following the road, and then at the Parting Stone, the landmark that pointed travelers toward one direction or another, he turned north toward Lexington. A few miles removed from the guardhouse, Dawes rode over the wet earth of the Muddy River, the brooks and water pools and tall grass there, and into Brookline. Three more miles on, and freer now to gallop, to make haste, Dawes crossed the Charles River at its narrow point, clattering over the wood-planked bridge, the Great Bridge, into Cambridge.

Now Dawes was near Harvard Square, maybe seven miles from the guardhouse and still nine miles from the house of Reverend Clarke. In Cambridge he may have paused to alert someone of the British troops' activity and of his errand to Lexington. Soon, townspeople came and removed the wooden planks from the Great Bridge, meaning to slow any redcoats who might try to cross there, as the next morning they would.

Dawes rode out of Cambridge and up into Menotomy, crossing the moonlit brook. The road wended northwest and became rocky along its sides, and then Dawes's route joined the same road that Revere had ridden that night and that the British soldiers had ridden before him, the main westward route to the center of Lexington.

He had traveled by necessity a longer route than Revere's and had ridden more slowly, but Dawes would complete his journey unharmed.

Two hundred and twenty-five years after the night of the Ride, Malcolm Gladwell, in *The Tipping Point,* tried to explain why Revere on his ride ignited such a wide response, Minutemen activated in one area after another, while Dawes on his ride stirred hardly any activity at all—the removal of the Great Bridge planks notwithstanding. Few Patriots from the towns and areas that Dawes passed through made it to the sites of the battles on April 19. There are no reports of militia leaders or other riders having been spurred by receiving news from Dawes.

The most compelling of Gladwell's conclusions—conclusions that he came to in part by drawing parallels to other instances of messages being conveyed by word of mouth—is that Revere succeeded in large part due to his social manner, the ease with which he interacted with other people. A *connector* is the Gladwell-coined term. Revere not only knew many people along his route, Isaac Hall among them, he also had the demeanor to size up and engage a new person, Martin Herrick as an example, and press upon the person the news.

Revere's network of friends and acquaintances extended as far and as widely as just about anyone else's.

He was an active, long-standing Mason. He was part of the politically powerful North End Caucus. He attended pre-Revolutionary meetings of the Long Room Club. He joined with others in painted face and helped pull off the Boston Tea Party. He ran an active shop on a busy street near a bustling wharf, a shop frequented by any number of customers with any number of dispositions. He rode one critical Committee of Correspondence mission after another. Revere liked talking to people, he liked making his point known. He liked to feel that his words and actions had consequences, and he liked being an agent of change.

Both Dawes and Revere carried the same news and were presumably given the same assignment by Joseph Warren. Dawes was a passionate Patriot, imaginative, dedicated, courageous, and talented in his way. He was not nearly so close to the heart of the resistance as Revere was—few people were—but on that night Dawes bore information that would change the life of anyone it was impressed upon.

Revere, not knowing what might yet befall him in the night and early morning ahead, galloped into Lexington having left behind him a countryside ablaze with activity. Dawes, when he arrived at Reverend Clarke's house some thirty minutes after Revere did, left behind him only a bit of rustling to disturb the still of night.

* * *

Revere tied up Brown Beauty and went into the house. He was splattered with mud, his face flushed, his breath heavy from the exertion of the ride. Revere told Hancock and Samuel Adams about the British troops, how hundreds of them had left over the water to Cambridge hours earlier. It was understood that Adams and Hancock could now be in real jeopardy. Reverend Clarke feared that when the greater group of British forces arrived, "sudden arrest, if not assassination, might be attempted." The parson's house was full, with his wife, Lucy, and their children, as well as the aunt and the fiancée of Hancock, stirring now in the bedrooms upstairs.

"After I had been there about half an hour, Mr. Dawes came," Revere recalled. "We refreshed ourselves and set off for Concord to secure the stores."

Word spread through Lexington, to the Minutemen already assembled at the Buckman Tavern and then by foot messenger to the houses surrounding the town. A fellow militiaman "called me out of my bed and said the British troops had left Boston and were on their march to Lexington," said John Munroe, a twenty-seven-year-old corporal in the Lexington militia. "I immediately repaired to the place of parade, which was the common adjoining the meetinghouse, where sixty or seventy of the company had assembled in arms."

At house after house men were woken and roused, and from house after house to the common they came. Soon the church bells would ring, and the signal guns would fire so that the wider countryside should know.

Revere and Dawes were long hours into the night's mission and twenty hours or more removed from their last sleep. To refresh themselves, to rejuvenate, they might have bent over a basin and laved water on their faces and necks. They might have eaten something warm and taken a drink of coffee. They would have watered and tended their horses before remounting and continuing on the westward road to Concord.

What may have been said aloud at Buckman Tavern, and what the militia leaders there certainly recognized, was that the three men—Solomon Brown, Jonathan Loring, Elijah Sanderson—who had left from the tavern along that road hours before, aiming to stalk the British soldiers on patrol, had not returned.

"We started probably about nine o'clock," Elijah Sanderson recalled. This was maybe an hour after the officers had passed through Lexington, before Joseph Warren had even summoned Revere to his home in Boston, before the magnitude of the redcoat movement was known in the Middlesex towns. "The fears were that their object was to come back in the night and seize Hancock and Adams and carry them into Boston."

The three young Patriots rode out carefully on the soft

earth, keeping to the shadows. The road widened as it emerged out of Lexington. It passed through stretches of woodland and fenced farmland, with homes and barns along the way.

About three miles along the way to Concord, Lexington gave way to the town of Lincoln. Here the road was sometimes called the Great North Road. When the British officers rode there that night, they made enough disturbance that they woke forty-eight-year-old Josiah Nelson, who came suddenly out of his house still partly in nightclothes to find out what was happening.

Nelson owned good land on both sides of the Concord Road—including more than forty working acres of tillage, plowland. and mowed meadow, as well as an acre of planted orchard land. Along with Nelson's house two barns stood on the property. Well back from either side of the road, wooded areas ran along his northernmost and southernmost acres. Nelson, a committed Patriot and the youngest of three siblings living nearby, had been buying and cultivating land in and around Lincoln for many years. This was land he had every motivation to protect.

By now a level of apprehension and fear may have crept into the minds of the British officers. A few local loyalists, rare in these parts, had joined them on foot, acting as guides along the route. Still, this was a small group moving through an area thick with Patriots hot for conflict. The officers had been talking among themselves about how big the populations of these towns were, which was another way of asking how many potential enemies surrounded them.

When Nelson rushed up and asked who the riders were and why they were out, one of the British officers hit him abruptly with a sword, opening a gash near the top of Nelson's skull. The men surrounded Nelson, then threatened him and warned him to keep silent about seeing them and about the officer having hit him. After a time, the officers freed Nelson to go back into his home, where his wife, Elizabeth, tended to his wound. The Nelsons had been married for twenty-four years and had no children.

When Elizabeth was done bandaging the gash, Josiah tacked and mounted his mare. He first rode eastward on the Great North Road, then turned left onto a bridle path and rode that narrow way through unmown fields the two miles north to Bedford, to deliver news that the officers were not only out but were also—it was clear, just look at him—operating from a stance of aggression. Elizabeth in the meantime alerted some of the neighboring houses.

Now, as Elijah Sanderson, Solomon Brown, and Jonathan Loring rode slowly together through that portion of the road that ran through Josiah Nelson's land, and then beyond, all was quiet. They rode silently and soon passed near a stand of birch trees. Then, suddenly, across the body of the road, the shape of the British officers, high in their saddles, came into view. "One rode up and seized my bridle and another my arm," said Sanderson. "And one man put his pistol to my breast and told me that if I resisted, I was a dead man. I asked what he wanted. He replied he wanted to detain me a little while." Brown and Loring were also taken under control. The officers ordered all three of them to get off their horses and then led the horses away and hitched them to trees away from the road. Some of the British officers had also dismounted and, kicking aside some wooden fencing, led the three captives into a field, lit brightly by the moon.

"They examined and questioned us where we were going," said Sanderson. "Two of them stayed in the road, and the other seven with us, relieving each other from time to time. They put many questions to us, which I evaded. They kept us separately and treated us very civilly. They particularly inquired where Hancock and Adams were; also about the population. One said, 'You've been numbering the inhabitants, haven't ye?' I told him how many it was reported there were."

During the time that the officers kept Sanderson and Brown and Loring captive, Revere reached Lexington, and so did Dawes. And now Revere and Dawes were together, up on their mounts, and had begun to ride along that same road toward Concord.

* * *

THEY RODE OUT past Buckman Tavern and past the Lexington Common and picked up the big road heading west. They moved at an intentional pace and planned to alert the houses on their way once they got outside town. Quite soon, as Revere told it, he and Dawes "were overtaken by a young gentleman named Prescott, who belonged to Concord and was going home." Samuel Prescott was a twenty-three-year-old doctor from a family line of doctors, and he knew the area well from making house calls. On this night Dr. Prescott was returning not from a professional appointment but from a personal one, with a young woman who lived near the Munroe Tavern in Lexington.

Revere regarded Prescott, spoke with him, and determined that he was a "high son of liberty." Prescott volunteered to help Revere and Dawes deliver the alarm. Prescott said, Revere would recall, "He would stop with either of us, for the people between there and Concord knew him and would give the more credit to what we said."

Maybe a mile and a half out of Lexington the three riders rode through land owned by Ebeneezer Fiske, land that had been in the Fiske family for better than 125 years. The sprawling acreage accommodated the Fiske home, a barn, and a corn shed, as well as fenced grounds for livestock and several wells. Fiske, elderly and confined to bed, held enslaved people, and these enslaved people would have worked and maintained the prosperous land.

Here the road to Concord rose, climbing Fiske Hill, and then bent northward, away from the Fiske farmland. Low pine trees lined the southern edge of the road, and the other trees, paper birches and white oak, were bare or just beginning to bud. With little leaf coverage, the wide road lay moonlit nearly all the way across. Revere, Dawes, and Prescott may have delivered the alarm to someone at the Fiske house, the Whittemore house, the Hastings house. Exactly which houses, and exactly who in those houses they alarmed, Revere would always be loath to say, keeping that in secrecy as a kind of protection. The heavy sense of the severity and danger of what the Patriots were engaged in—rising treasonously against Royal governance—clung to Revere as it clung to many who were active in that time. Even when he gave his later account of the Ride, twenty-three years later, Revere wanted to be identified anonymously, simply as a Son of Liberty.

The road dipped and then flattened. Stone walls ran through some of the surrounding property, and large individual boulders stood in some places. Revere, Dawes, and Prescott crossed the Lexington-Lincoln line onto the Great North Road. Now there were hills around them and more trees closer to the road. They were a little less than three miles from the Lexington Common, and a little more than four miles from the center of Concord. "Mr. Dawes and the doctor stopped to alarm the people of a house," Revere would recall. He continued to ride ahead, alone. He got about one hundred yards in front of the other two, then two hundred yards, three hundred and more. And then, just before him, Revere spotted two mounted British officers under trees at the side of the road, "in nearly the same situation as those officers were near Charlestown."

Revere said, "In an instant I was surrounded by four officers. They had placed themselves in a straight road that inclined each way. They had taken down a pair of bars on the north side of the road, and two of them were under a tree in the pasture."

"God damn you, stop!" one of the officers bellowed. "If you go an inch further, you are a dead man."

Prescott, hearing the noise, rode up brandishing the butt end of his whip. He and Revere hustled forward and tried without success to forge a way through or around the line of officers. A couple of them had their guns out, and at least one had drawn his sword. Dawes had not yet appeared from behind them. The officers forced Revere and Prescott into the pastureland off the road, and then Prescott suddenly bolted, leaping a low stone wall, galloping into an open meadow, free and unfollowed and headed toward Concord riding the backland and byways he had known all his life.

Now, the officers spotted Dawes coming up along the road. Two of them made straight for him, and he swiftly turned and rode eastward toward Lexington. The officers pursued him off the road and into a farmyard, where Dawes, practiced in the art of deception, called out as he neared the house, "Come on, boys, I've got two of them!" The officers, frightened that they'd been ensnared into a Patriot trap, pulled away and charged back toward the others. Something in the tumult spooked Dawes's horse. He reared and pitched abruptly, throwing Dawes into the mud violently enough that Dawes's timepiece flew from his pocket. The horse galloped off and Dawes, shaken but unhurt, left the scene on foot, away from the officers and Revere, hoping to find another mount and to ride on to somewhere else and continue delivering the alarm.

In the commotion of Prescott's flourish and the brief chase after Dawes, Revere saw not far from him an area of woodland. He broke toward it, "intending when I reached that to jump my horse and run afoot." It's hard to shoot a man who is dodging among the trees. Instead, at the edge of the wood, Revere came up short. "When I got there, out started six officers, on horseback, and they ordered me to dismount."

Immediately the officers interrogated Revere. How long had he been out on the road? Where was he coming from? Was he an express rider? What was his mission? As Revere answered—that he had come from Boston hours earlier, that he had alerted the countryside along his way, that he and all whom he had told were keen to the troops of redcoats bound for Lexington and Concord, and, most chillingly, that by now hundreds of Patriots were surely headed this way—the faces of the officers began to pale in the yellow light of the moon.

Said one, "Sir, may I crave your name?"

"Revere."

"What? Paul Revere?"

"Yes."

Not every British officer would have known Paul Revere's face. But all of them knew his name. They knew he was at the center of the opposition, an enemy to the Crown. They knew he had caused trouble for their operations more than once before. The officers brayed insults at Revere and spoke to him threateningly, and then the leader of the group, Major Edward Mitchell, "clapped his pistol to my head," said Revere, "and told me that he was going to ask me some questions, and if I did not give him true answers, he would blow my brains out." The other captives, Sanderson, Brown. and Loring, watched from the edge of the trees, barely fifteen feet away.

Mitchell searched Revere, ensuring that he was unarmed, and then asked him again about where he had been and what he had done that night, pressing him for more detail. "I was not afraid," Revere said. He answered Mitchell brashly, confidently, and truthfully.

"I heard him speak up with energy to them, 'Gentlemen, you've missed your aim!'" Sanderson recalled. "One said rather hardly, 'What of our aim?' Revere replied, 'I came out of Boston an hour after your troops had come out of Boston and landed at Lechmere's Point, and if I had not known people had been sent out to give information to the country, and time enough to get fifty miles, I would have ventured one shot from you before I would have suffered you to have stopped me.'"

The officers, agitated now, spooked and troubled by what Revere had said, moved close together to discuss their next action. There seemed little point staying on patrol. Major Mitchell ordered Revere to get back onto his horse and ordered Sanderson, Brown, and Loring to mount their horses as well. Major Mitchell led Revere and Brown Beauty into the road, and an officer mounted to the right of Revere took hold of Brown Beauty's reins. One thing the Royal officers knew about Revere was that he could really ride a horse. "By God, sir, you are not to ride with reins, I assure you," Major Mitchell said to Revere.

The officers brought Sanderson, Brown, and Loring into the road behind Revere, encircling the three men on all sides, and the whole group began to ride toward Lexington. After a short distance Major Mitchell told one of his sergeants to take over the control of Revere's reins and gave the sergeant a simple command: if he tries to break free, or if he insults you, shoot him. The sergeant kept his pistol pointed at Revere at all times.

In this fashion the group traveled toward Lexington.

The officers badgered Revere indiscriminately as they rode, making personal remarks, calling him a "rebel," and not meaning it in a nice way. "You're in a damned critical situation," one officer said.

The group picked up speed, and when Sanderson's small horse began to lag, one of the officers struck it with the flat side of his sword. The riders passed the Josiah Nelson property and passed the Fiske farmland, returning to Lexington just the way they all had come. "When we got within a half mile of the meetinghouse, we heard a gun fired," Revere recalled. "The major asked me what it was for. I told him it was to alarm the country."

Then from Lexington the church bells rang. "The bells a-ringing, the town's alarmed, and you're all dead men," Jonathan Loring blurted out. It was well past two o'clock in the morning.

The officers stopped and again conferred with one another. The four captive men sat on their shifting horses waiting, powerless and uncertain, like passengers in a stalled carriage or aboard a ship bobbing within sight of land. They knew there was a chance the Regulars would kill them.

One of the officers dismounted and ordered Sanderson, Brown, and Loring to dismount as well. "I must do you an injury," the officer said. With his sword he cut the bridle and girth from Sanderson's horse. Then he cut the bridle and girth from Brown's horse—the horse Brown had borrowed from Reverend Clarke—and from Loring's horse, and the three horses were all loose and could canter away from the road and away from where they'd heard the gunshots and the bell ringing. The officers told the three men they were free. Revere they kept, and with him the officers rode at a trot, highly alert, toward the center of Lexington. Sanderson, Brown, and Loring turned off the road and headed by shortcut toward the meetinghouse, "through the swamp, through the mud and water," Sanderson said. They hoped to reach the meetinghouse before the officers did.

"I asked the major to dismiss me," said Revere. "He said he would carry me, let the consequence be what it will." Soon the group got close to the meetinghouse, within clear sight of it. At that same moment some of the militiamen, meaning to further rouse their compatriots in the outlying areas, fired from outside the Buckman Tavern, as Revere remembered, "a volley of guns, which appeared to alarm the officers very much. The major ordered us to halt. He asked me how far it was to Cambridge and whether there was any other road."

That quickly the officers feared for their lives, saw just how vulnerable they were. Being captured by armed militia could mean serious trouble. Being captured while keeping Paul Revere as their prisoner would almost certainly mean their end. "The major asked the sergeant if his horse was tired, he said yes," Revere recalled.

"Take that man's horse," Major Mitchell told the sergeant.

Revere was ordered off Brown Beauty, and the sergeant swung himself up onto her back and for a moment settled himself there. Another officer cut the bridle and girth of the sergeant's horse, and that horse was now also free to run away from the noise and the commotion and into the open fields. Then, leaving Revere, the officers galloped off through Lexington and out, speeding in the direction of Cambridge, eager to find and join the Royal troops.

Sanderson, Brown, and Loring were themselves nearing the meetinghouse—they had seen from a distance the officers stop and free Revere, and then go galloping away. Sanderson walked to Buckman Tavern, where, he later recalled, the "citizens were coming and going." The scene now buzzed with anticipation and preparation—the testing of small arms, the stashing of family silver. Everyone wondered exactly when the troops of redcoats might march up. At times a scout galloped eastward on the road, toward Menotomy, to see if the troops were close. There was still no sign of them. "I went into the tavern," Sanderson recalled, "and, after a while, went to sleep in my chair by the fire."

There would be no sleep, not anytime soon, for Revere. With Brown Beauty gone, he continued on foot. "I went across the burying ground," Revere recalled, "and some pastures and came to the Reverend Mr. Clarke's house, where I found Messrs. Hancock and Adams."

THE BLEMISH ON the long after-Ride life of Paul Revere—a life defined by his remarkable professional resourcefulness and success; by his constant, loving relationship with his wife, Rachel; by the affection of his children and by the honor and friendships he accrued in his public and private life—came in the summer of 1779 when Revere, as a lieutenant colonel commanding one hundred men, took part in the disastrous naval expedition at Penobscot Bay, Maine. The American effort in Penobscot Bay, one thousand soldiers strong, was undone by its leaders' disorganization, poor cooperation, and ill planning. All ships were lost, and the British held on to the land. Afterward the American commander of the expedition, Dudley Saltonsall, received a court-martial and was found guilty of ineptitude. Revere was charged with cowardice.

Cowardice is not a description lightly pinned on anyone, nor does it seem at all consistent with the general temperament and behavior of Paul Revere. Rather than endure the cost and indignity of the charges—charges that forced him to relinquish his naval post—Revere fought immediately against them. He termed the accusations malicious, false, and unfair. "What is more dear to me than life: my character," Revere wrote. He petitioned, and then petitioned again, to be court-martialed so that the case against him, and in effect his name, might come to trial. In February of 1782, it did. Revere was fully acquitted. "The court, considering that the whole Army was in great Confusion and so scattered and dispersed that no regular Orders were or could be given," the judgment read, "are of the Opinion that Lt. Col. Revere be acquitted with equal Honor as the other Officers in the same expedition."

What became clear during those and earlier proceedings is that whatever military errors Revere made in Penobscot Bay—and he certainly made errors—the counts against him had stemmed largely from a clash of personalities. Revere had about him an arrogance, his fellow leaders said, that neither sat well with them nor served the mission. Revere scornfully described an early strategy meeting of the American commanders as "more like a meeting in a Coffee House than a council of War." And he conveyed disdain for some of his peers throughout the expedition. Major William Todd wrote of Revere at Penobscot Bay, "His absolute harangue . . . always overpowered those more mildly disposed. His blustering rhetoric, which ever arose from his absolute arbitrary notions and false conceit of his superior genius was one of the causes of delay."

This alleged breach seems more plausible, far more so than cowardice. Even before the night of the Ride, Revere was self-possessed. Confident, cocksure, proud of his own judgment and his own intuition. Imagine how the events of April 18 and April 19, 1775, might have further buttressed the ego of such a man. He executed a near-flawless alarm, deftly eluding would-be captors to complete a mission that defined the beginning of the American Revolution. When later captured by an armed, aggressive enemy, Revere's courage and brashness—*I heard him speak up with energy to them,* said Sanderson. *I was not afraid,* said Revere—helped secure not only his own improbable freedom but the freedom of three other men. That sequence of events most conceivably could have honed an edge of arrogance to his demeanor, to his life ahead. Hale fellow in the tavern. Uncompromising in the time of action.

Nor was Revere's night complete after he had escaped the Royal officers and their trained pistols. Revere's fellow riders rode on elsewhere. Prescott critically delivered the alarm to Concord, then continued to Acton and Snow. He dispatched his brother, Abel, to ride to Sudbury and Framingham. Dawes, local whispers suggested, may have found another horse and taken the alarm to points south of Lexington. Revere during this time took himself back to the heart of it all, to Lexington, where the pressure sat and to where the battle would soon arrive. He had it in his mind to do whatever he could to ensure that Samuel Adams and John Hancock—the human pillars holding up the New England resistance—were kept safe from harm.

AT REVEREND CLARKE'S house Revere told Adams and Hancock all that had happened, and "I told them of my treatment," he said. That Adams and Hancock were still at the house, still in Lexington, hours after Revere had made clear the imminence of the British troops, felt troubling. It was because of Hancock, who refused to leave, saying he planned to join with the Patriot militia on the Lexington Common and fight the redcoats hand to hand. When Revere came into the house, Hancock was cleaning his gun. Already that night he had sharpened his sword.

Adams sought to dissuade Hancock, resting a hand upon him. "That is not our business," Adams said. "We are in the cabinet." Clarke and Revere impressed upon Hancock his need to protect himself, that Hancock being killed or imprisoned would hurt the Revolution far more than his killing of a few British soldiers on the battlefield might help.

At last Hancock yielded and he and Adams set off, not on horseback but, per Adams, by chaise. A more comfortable ride, and with room for their essential belongings. They were bound for Woburn, for the parsonage there, a few miles northeast of Lexington. Revere went with them, as protection and support, and so did John Lowell, Hancock's clerk. Somewhere toward the end of the route, as they neared the parsonage in Woburn, Hancock and Lowell realized they had left something behind at the Buckman Tavern: Hancock's trunk. The trunk with so many essential, and incriminating, documents inside.

Hancock and Adams stayed in Woburn while Revere and Lowell returned quickly to Lexington. It was about four o'clock in the morning. They came to Reverend Clarke's house, where the Clarke family and Hancock's aunt Lydia and Hancock's fiancée, Dorothy Quincy, still waited, awake and concerned. Nothing there had changed. "An elderly man came in," Revere recalled. "He said he had just come from the tavern, that a man had come from Boston, who said there were no British troops coming."

Revere and Lowell left Clarke's house and were walking toward Buckman Tavern when they met another man, a rider, "on a full gallop who told us the troops were coming up the rocks," Revere would recall. "We afterwards met another who said they were close by."

Even as Revere and Lowell arrived at the tavern and then went inside, militiamen were coming out, headed for the far end of the Lexington Green to prepare for the British troops. Revere and Lowell climbed the narrow staircase off the tavern entranceway—first one switchback and then another—and came to the second floor, to the Buckmans' bedroom, where the trunk was. From the window, you could face east toward the lightening sky and you could look down over the open road that came into Lexington from Menotomy, the road that began miles away at the river.

And then Revere saw them, a sudden, moving mass along the road, the Regulars of His Majesty's Royal Army in full uniformed splendor, "very near, upon a full march." The troops had the day's first light at their backs. Their firearms were visible, their bayonets clear. They were solemn in their march—orderly, intent, menacing—a thick red band of men that stretched on and on for row after row after row. The soldiers' footfalls, partly muted through the window glass, landed rhythmically on the damp earth, one collective thump after another.

Major Mitchell had joined with the troops. He rode near John Pitcairn, the army major who had quartered beside Revere in the North End those many months, and who was now leading his detachment of marines at the head of the column. Lieutenant Colonel Francis Smith, the commander of the operation, rode toward the back.

Revere gripped the metal handle on one side of John Hancock's trunk and Lowell the handle on the other side. Three feet long, nearly two feet deep, twenty-four inches from its flat bottom to its rounded top—bulky and solidly built. The trunk handles worked into their palms as they descended the narrow staircase, maneuvering the switchbacks, and came again to the landing by the tavern's heavy front door. Then Revere and Lowell opened the door and stepped outside.

The sound of the march was now much louder, and so were the sounds from the farther edge of the Green, the beating of a drum and the voices of men shouting urgently to one another. Morning had arrived, a soft, clear early light. Revere and Lowell began to move away from the tavern and toward Reverend Clarke's house a few hundred yards or more past the Green. Clarke was out on his property looking toward the common while the others from the household watched from the windows upstairs. The Patriot militia had gathered in and near the meetinghouse, a place of refuge on other days, but today the building that held the powder. The men inside were loading their guns.

Hancock's trunk, filled with thick papers and notes, letters and ledgers, had some weight to it, though Revere and Lowell did not pause to put it down. They made their way onto the green, onto the dew-dampened spring lawn, and carried the trunk through the assemblage of wide-eyed Patriot militia "to the number as I suppose of fifty or sixty," said Revere. There were older men among the militia and there were men barely past boyhood. There were landowners, saddlers, field-workers, and hired hands. Gentry of a kind and commoners. There were white men and Black men. Husbands, fathers, brothers, sons. William Munroe. Solomon Brown. Prince Estabrook. Elijah

Sanderson. Scores more. Munroe, under the direction of Captain John Parker, had the militia organized into two cohesive lines.

Revere and Lowell had gotten about one hundred yards away when the British troops, as Revere recalled, "appeared on both sides of the meetinghouse." These were troops at the vanguard, who had broken out from the main column. Major Pitcairn rode briefly out onto the green. Patriot captain John Parker, seeing the numbers against them, ordered the militiamen to break from their lines and disperse. For all the zeal among many in the Patriot militia and among many in the Royal Army, neither side wanted to be the first to fire on the other. Neither side wanted the immovable weight of having started something that could not be undone.

The Patriot drumming had stopped, and the shouting from the soldiers diminished. A wariness settled on the green, as each side regarded the other. An underlying silence. After the long hard night just past, and after all the tension of the months and years before, here was the tentative new day. Here was the start of a future that both sides could see.

No one paid mind to Revere and Lowell as they shuffled ahead with Hancock's trunk. Some of the militiamen were standing out in the open, and others had set themselves behind stone walls. They wore farmer's pants and their workday shirts, and some of them had their guns raised. Some among the British soldiers, clad in their buttons and caps, had their muskets pointed back at the militia. The mounted officers drew their pistols.

Reverend Clarke's house lay ahead of Revere and Lowell, and there waited the carriage that would take Hancock's trunk to Woburn. Seven hours earlier Revere had left from Joseph Warren's doorway, and over those seven hours his life and the shape of the American future had forever changed. Revere was forty years old, and without sleep, and as alive as he had ever been. And then, from the side of him, from where he and Lowell had been moments before, Revere heard a sudden and violent report, a sound like a thousand reins snapping, a clap of bloody thunder, a gunshot at the dawn of day.

Henry Wadsworth Longfellow

14

LONGFELLOW

APRIL 1860

THE POET HENRY WADSWORTH LONGFELLOW climbed first the wooden stairs and then the mounted ladders inside the tower of the Old North Church, toward the belfry above. The many pigeons—"innumerable," Longfellow would say—perched on the wooden beams startled at Longfellow's ascent, and when they fluttered off, their beating wings echoed noisily within the tower. Longfellow was there with George Sumner, the brother of Charles Sumner, who was a U.S. senator from Massachusetts, a fierce abolitionist, and for many years Longfellow's most beloved friend.

From the window of the belfry, the two men could look out over the burial grounds and across the channel to Charlestown. Turning westward they took in the roofs of the town, leading out to Cambridge and toward Longfellow's house. He and his wife, Fanny, had five children, ages five to sixteen. On the broad lawn of their home Longfellow sometimes pushed the younger children in a wheelbarrow. He and Fanny read them books—recently *Don Quixote*—and took them to the theater. He rowed with his children on the freshwater pond and wrote in his diary about the delight of attending their costume parties. He comforted and guided his children in an active way. "It was always to my father that we went in our childish troubles," his son Ernest would say.

Longfellow and George Sumner made their way upward to the steeple of the Old North Church. It was April 5, 1860, a time of heavy unrest in the nation, unrest over the issue of enslaved people. Longfellow in that time attended what were called Anti-Slavery meetings to protest enslavement. He regularly gave money to buy the freedom of enslaved people. He donated to Black churches and schools and, earlier, in 1843, had published *Poems on Slavery,* which rebuked enslavers (albeit in gentle, poetic terms) as immoral. A few weeks before this visit to the Old North

Church, Longfellow had gone to a reading of *Othello* and the next day wrote in his diary, "A gloomy day; out of spirits. Hearing tragedies is not cheering to the heart of man."

Although Longfellow was not generally public with his political concerns, he recognized enslavement as an existential sin, and his attention to the present and developing conflict in America was keen. "Even now as I write they are leading John Brown to execution in Virginia for attempting to rescue slaves!" he had noted in his diary in December of 1859. "This is sowing the wind to reap the whirlwind which will come soon." A few years earlier, Longfellow reeled, then angered, when Charles Sumner was physically beaten on the floor of the Senate by a pro-enslavement representative incensed by Sumner's speech "The Barbarism of Slavery." In a letter to the convalescent Sumner, Longfellow wrote, "A brave and noble speech you made; never to die out in the memories of men!" Then added, "It is the greatest voice on the greatest subject that has been uttered since we became a nation. . . . You have torn the mask off the traitors; and at last the spirit of the North is aroused."

April 5, 1860, was a Thursday and had, in Boston, been designated a day of fasting and prayer. Businesses were closed. Many people attended church in the morning, and in the afternoon many more mingled on the streets. It was a lovely, sunny day, touched, in the language of Longfellow, by the early foam of spring.

In choosing to make this outing to the North End, some five miles on foot from his home, and to explore the Old North Church, Longfellow and George Sumner were of course aware of what had unfolded there nearly eighty-five years earlier, on April 18, 1775. The facts and the legend of that night—what it might represent as a story about rallying to a purpose at high personal risk, and of accepting individual responsibility and agency—provided rich narrative grist. At a time when the morality and future of the nation felt at stake, a time that would call for the courage and response of the people, the story of Paul Revere was a story a poet such as Longfellow could use.

WHAT LONGFELLOW CHOSE as a poetic subject made an impact far beyond the corridors of his own thought or the musings of a literary elite. He was fifty-three years old. He had written the epic poems *Evangeline* and *The Song of Hiawatha*. And he was the most successful and widely read poet in America.

Paul Revere's mission, the signals from the Old North Church, and all that happened in and around Boston at the start of the American Revolution were highly resonant to Longfellow. He was born and raised in Portland and had attended Bowdoin College in Maine. He had lived in Cambridge since 1837, in a house where George

Washington had headquartered during the Siege of Boston in July of 1775. During the Revolution, Longfellow's grandfather Peleg Wadsworth fought alongside Revere at the Battle of Penobscot Bay.

When Charles Dickens came to America in 1842, Longfellow, then thirty-four, spent a full day out with him in Boston, serving as a guide. They walked past the wharves where the tea had been tossed into the harbor. They walked up through the North End and along Salem Street to the Old North Church. They looked at the burial grounds and then continued downhill and walked across Commercial Street, then across the bridge into Charlestown. This was an exceptionally memorable day for Longfellow. He described the experience as "glorious" and the day proved to be the setting-off point for a lifelong friendship, and a mutual professional and personal admiration, between Dickens and himself.

Longfellow knew the particulars of Revere's ride perhaps better than most. In 1832, long before his fame and success, he published a sonnet and part of a novel in *New England Magazine.* The sonnet appeared just next to a piece on Revere that included a reprinting of the definitive account of that night in Revere's own words. Longfellow remembered these pages and perhaps kept them. In 1877, forty-five years after it appeared and seventeen years after Longfellow had written and published the poem "Paul Revere's Ride," Longfellow instructed a curious reader that this old edition of *New England Magazine* was a place to find Revere's account.

The details of the ride provided a framework for Longfellow and not, to the benefit of both the work and generations of readers, a limitation. It was during the 1860 visit to the Old North Church that Longfellow drew the last inspiration for his great narrative poem. He began writing it the following day, April 6. On April 19 (the anniversary of the early morning when Revere's ride came to an end) he alluded in his diary to some progress: "I wrote a few lines in 'Paul Revere's Ride'; this being the day of that achievement." On December 20, 1860, the very same day that South Carolina became the first of seven pro-enslavement states to secede from the Union, "Paul Revere's Ride" appeared in *The Atlantic.* Modern scholars, notably the Harvard historian Jill Lepore, have observed how the language in "Paul Revere's Ride" echoes language in *Poems on Slavery,* an intentional evocation.

Whether the poem was read as a parable for the founding of the nation, or for the urgency of a response in the foreshadow of the Civil War, it made and left an extraordinary mark. Later in life Longfellow received from admirers and grateful readers gifts relating to Revere. After being given in 1871 a silver spoon that had been forged by Revere, Longfellow wrote in thanks, "When I received it, I felt as if I had been christened over again and had an 'apostle spoon' sent me as a present. Paul Revere was an apostle of liberty, if not of religion."

And the poem has of course far outlived its author, surviving as one of America's most beloved and known poems, sometimes read by parents to children and ample in its allegorical weight. "Listen, my children, and you shall hear / Of the midnight ride of Paul Revere" are the poem's famous opening lines. The stanzas lead through an imagined version of the ride, elevated by couplets such as "One if by land, and two if by sea; / And I on the opposite shore will be."

For its content, its allusions, and its ethos, the poem continued and continues to bear relevance to any number of modern contexts, perspectives, and movements. In the early 2000s, during budget hearings on the floor of the U.S. Senate, Senator Edward Kennedy of Massachusetts recited "Paul Revere's Ride" from memory to West Virginia senator Robert Byrd, the chair of the Appropriations Committee, who recited it back.

Before Longfellow wrote and published "Paul Revere's Ride," not a single book of American biographical sketches—and several of them came out in the 1800s—included an entry for Paul Revere. He has appeared in every such or similar book since.

On April 18, 1875, one hundred years after Paul Revere sprang to his saddle, and when Longfellow was sixty-eight and suffering from neuralgia, he wrote in his diary, "In the evening my girls drive over to Prospect Hill to see the lighting of Paul Revere's lanterns in the belfry of the old North Church." A few days later he wrote to his friend George Washington Greene, "For the next few years we shall have centennial celebrations all over the country. I hope they will do some good; and I think they may, in holding up the noble lives of other days as examples."

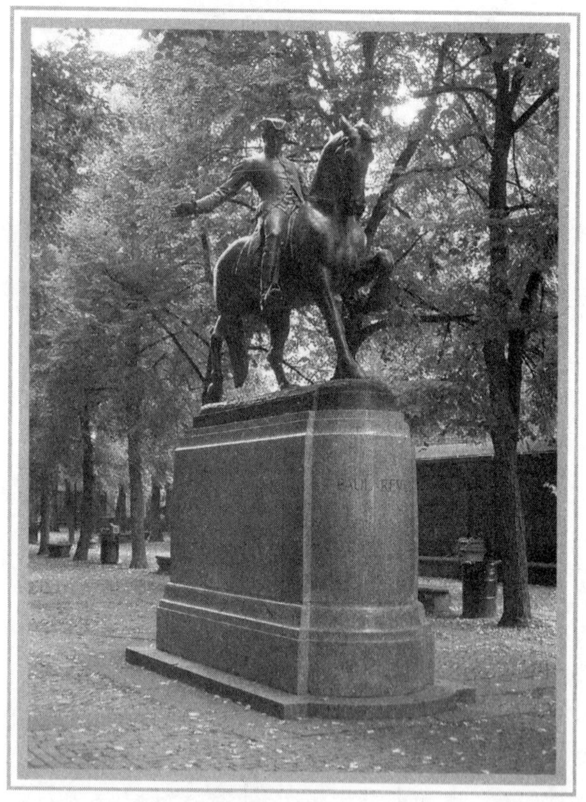

Statue of Paul Revere, Boston

15

ECHOES

NOT A DAY ON EARTH PASSES WITHOUT THE name and figure of Paul Revere being mentioned, alluded to, and invoked. That's not just because of the branding—there's a town and beach named for him outside Boston; there are Paul Revere schools and academies in states from coast to coast. What keeps Revere and his remarkable ride so present in the nation's collective "remembrance" and knowledge of the time, so rooted in the American psyche, so much a part of America's self-told story, is the clear and simple message the story conveys, in its essence, its symbolism and its fact.

You can apply Revere and his story as you might.

In recent years a political group in Michigan, the Manistee Tea Party, developed a program on "citizen journalism training," which it called Operation Paul Revere. A bit before that, the global news collaborative Covering Climate Now published a cartoon of activist Greta Thunberg riding horseback sounding the alarm with a lantern in her hand and called her "today's Paul Revere." Both the scientist James Hansen and the former U.S. vice president Al Gore have been called the Paul Revere of climate change. In 2024, Abby Abildness, a leader in the New Apostolic Reformation group, embraced the mantle of "Pennsylvania's Paul Revere" as she sought to spread a message of Christian supremacy across that state. There's a Paul Revere's pizza chain in Iowa, so named to emphasize its speed and dependability in delivery. An advertisement for Mint Mobile that features the actor Ryan Reynolds also deploys Paul Revere's great-great-great-great-granddaughter Avery Revere, who delivers the lines "Unlimited is coming. Unlimited is coming." In 1971, Vietnam protesters devised a plan to begin at Lexington Green and march Paul Revere's route in reverse: the undoing of democracy.

Although it was a journey of fewer than twenty miles on known country road, Revere's ride has about it the veneer of adventure, exploration even. The bravery needed, the danger that lurked, and the impact of the mission's success are all implicit. He rose to the moment, putting an ideal, and a people, ahead of himself. Revere is one of the relatively few historical figures—akin in this way to Saint George, who slayed the dragon; to Pheidippides, who ran from Marathon to Athens; to Rosa Parks, who held her ground—linked definitively to one act. Proof that a single conscious act can change the world, and one's place within it.

"You could possibly make the case that the biggest impact Paul Revere had on America was later in life when he rolled the copper the country needed to fight the war of 1812," says Nina Zannieri, the executive director of the Paul Revere Memorial Association, which encompasses the Paul Revere House. "But that's not what people generally want to talk about. They want to talk about the Ride."

The Paul Revere House draws more than 250,000 visitors a year from all over the country and the world. On significant years, and 2025 is one, it might draw close to 325,000. Each year the USS *Constitution* brings graduates of its chief petty officers' training program to Paul Revere House, where they gather in the courtyard and sing "Anchors Aweigh." The house stands as the oldest remaining residence anywhere in downtown Boston. Inside and out it looks essentially as it looked 250 years ago, on the night when Paul Revere stood within its walls, donned his overcoat, pulled on his boots, and headed out toward the Charles River and then to a horse on the opposite shore.

In 1782, a year reverberant with the ongoing shocks and aftershocks of the American Revolution and when American victory and independence began to appear inevitable, David Brown, a fifty-year-old Concord landowner, bought from the Old North Church one of the lanterns that Robert Newman had displayed, per Paul Revere's instruction, from the steeple chamber. This was not because Brown needed a light for the Concord chapel. In 1775 he had been captain of a Concord minuteman company, and now he wanted a piece of history, an artifact. The Brown family kept the lantern for sixty years, then passed it to a local collector. That explains why you can see it today not in Boston's North End but on display at the Concord Museum more than nineteen miles from the Old North Church, in a town where the light from Newman's lanterns never shone, but where there's no doubt about what their flames ignited.

Soon after the ride, still in 1775, the Massachusetts Provincial Congress asked Revere to render an account of the events—largely in hopes that his testimony about the conflict at Lexington Green on the morning of April 19 would support the assertion that British troops had fired the first shot of the war. In 1798, Jeremy Belknap, the corresponding secretary of the then-fledgling Massachusetts Historical Society, asked Revere to provide, for posterity, a fuller remembrance of the night, which Revere did. This was a story, Belknap knew, worth preserving.

Around that same time, meaning more than six decades before Henry Wadsworth Longfellow vaulted Paul Revere from the annals of local history into the global imagination, the poet Ebenezer Stiles rendered a version of Revere's ride in verses he titled "Story of the Battle of Concord and Lexington and Revere's Ride Twenty Years Ago." Here, with some minor misspellings corrected, are the opening stanzas:

Story of the Battle of Concord and Lexington and Revere's Ride Twenty Years Ago

He spared neither horse nor whip nor spur
As he galloped through mud and mire
He thought of naught but "Liberty"
And the lanterns that hung from the spire
He raced his steed through field and wood
Nor turned to ford the river
But faced his horse to the foaming flood
They swam across together

He madly dashed o'er mountain and moor
Never slacked spur nor rein

Until with a shout he stood by the door
Of the church by Concord Green
"They come They come" he loudly cried
"They are marching their Legions this way
Prepare to meet them ye true and tried
They'll be here by Break of day"

The bells were run the drums were beat
The Militia attended the roll
Every face we meet in the street
Wears a determined Scowl
For this is the day all men expected
Yet none of us wanted to see
But now it had come no one rejected
Our Country's call of Liberty

To little objection, Stiles stretched the tale (Revere never reached Concord Green) and enhanced the ride with some inventive details. A "foaming flood"? A "mountain"? Longfellow in his time also took numerous factual liberties to the benefit of poetic storytelling. This time some people were less comfortable with the straying from accuracy. The William Dawes descendant Henry Ware Holland expressed his dissatisfaction with Longfellow's rendering in his 1876 essay "William Dawes and His Ride with Paul Revere," in which, as Longfellow observed,

Holland "convicts me of high historic crimes and misdemeanors."

Holland is among a strain of intergenerational descendants, historians, and other history-minded folks who might be called the Defenders of William Dawes. In the 1970s some of them formed the Descendants of William Dawes Who Rode Association with the intent to elevate Dawes's historical stature. Their abiding complaint is that Revere's midnight mission has been unduly hailed while Dawes's has been criminally overlooked. Nina Zannieri encounters such people frequently. Not long ago she gave a talk on Revere's professional and personal life. As she finished, a hand shot up from the crowd. "He says, 'Why didn't you talk more about William Dawes?'" Zannieri recalled to me. To demonstrate her reaction to the question, Zannieri froze her face into a blank stare and let her clipboard fall clatteringly to the floor.

The Defenders of William Dawes have been at it since at least Holland's essay and, perhaps not surprisingly, there's a poem for this. In 1896 Helen F. Moore's send-up of Longfellow's "Paul Revere's Ride" appeared in *The Century Magazine.* Here it is:

The Midnight Ride of William Dawes

I am a wandering, bitter shade,
Never of me was a hero made;

Poets have never sung my praise,
Nobody crowned my brow with bays;
And if you ask me the fatal cause,
I answer only, "My name was Dawes."

'Tis all very well for the children to hear
Of the midnight ride of Paul Revere;
But why should my name be quite forgot,
Who rode as boldly and well, God wot?
Why should I ask? The reason is clear—
My name was Dawes and his Revere.

When the lights from the old North Church flashed
out,
Paul Revere was waiting about,
But I was already on my way.
The shadows of night fell cold and gray
As I rode, with never a break or a pause;
But what was the use, when my name was Dawes!

History rings with his silvery name;
Closed to me are the portals of fame.
Had he been Dawes and I Revere,
No one had heard of him, I fear.
No one has heard of me because
He was Revere and I was Dawes.

The poem's clearly a bit, and Moore plays it nicely. Though it's a bit that presents an actual axe to grind, then grinds it without logic or basis. As far as surname cachet, Dawes at the time of Longfellow's writing won hands down over Revere. And while the name Revere has the advantage of poetic resonance—not least because it summons the notion of reverence—the name Dawes is eminently rhymable. As the blogger J. L. Bell has pointed out, Will-iam Dawes is a near syllabic equivalent to Paul Re-vere. Hence the sonic success of Moore's parody. If we're to be at all serious in evaluating her jokey conclusion—*No one has heard of me because / He was Revere and I was Dawes*—remember that Revere's overall position in the Revolution was far more central than Dawes's was, and more specifically, Revere's ride that night appears to have been infinitely more impactful.

Revere's own narratives of the night are what made Dawes's ride more widely known. He honored Dawes and implied a debt to what Dawes had done. It was Revere who expressed concern to Samuel Adams and John Hancock when Dawes's arrival seemed delayed. Revere and Dawes were compatriots, unified by mission, fate, and belief. They chose to ride together toward Concord. It's because of Revere, and the attention that came to him, that many historians know of Dawes or his ride at all. Whatever quarrel the Defenders of William Dawes have, it is not with Revere. "Some of it is just gotcha culture; someone wants to tear someone down," says Zannieri. "It is certainly not a competition led by Paul Revere or by us. We love William Dawes. We love the fact that the Patriots were smart enough not to count on a single rider that night."

Still, it's not unreasonable for the Defenders of William Dawes to feel that Dawes deserves better recognition for his canniness and courage on the April 18, 1775. On firm principle and at great risk he put himself right into the mix. One might think of him as a kind of Robin to Revere's Batman.

Dr. Samuel Prescott, the rider who made it to Concord with even less continuing appreciation, hasn't engendered such a hue and cry for attention, although Prescott, like Dawes—and like just about anyone else known to history who rode a horse and delivered a message—draws comparisons to Paul Revere. That's inevitable—in the way that every violin is measured against a Stradivarius, every mountain peak against Everest.

This brings us to the case of Sybil Ludington. In April of 1777 at age sixteen, Ludington allegedly rode forty miles through parts of New York and Connecticut to rally militiamen against British troops who were aiming to seize a Continental Army supply depot in Danbury, Connecticut. Ludington's effort couldn't save Danbury: The Royal Army, facing little resistance, seized the supplies and destroyed much of the town. But her alert may have helped engage hundreds of militiamen, some of whom were under the leadership of her father, Colonel Henry Ludington, and helped force the British into retreat the following day.

Ludington's courage and perseverance over many long miles and through the dark of night have been lauded and celebrated over the past century. Neither she nor anyone else made a recorded mention of her ride during her lifetime (she died in 1839 at age seventy-seven), but an allusion to it appeared more than one hundred years after the fact in an 1880 book about the history of New York. That allusion was amplified with greater detail in a 1907 family memoir, which asserted, "There is no extravagance in comparing her ride with that of Paul Revere." Over the years the Ludington story began to gather steam.

In the 1930s roadside markers were placed at several points along her alleged route. (There's no record of exactly where she rode, but the markers serve as a best guess.) In 1961 a thrilling statue of Ludington—mounted high on her rearing horse and brandishing a stick above her head—went up in Carmel, New York, where Ludington completed her ride. A smaller version of the statue stands outside Danbury's public library. In 1975 Ludington appeared on a U.S. postage stamp as part of a series honoring overlooked heroes of the Revolutionary War.

More recently scholars have raised doubt as to whether Ludington's ride occurred. An analysis by the historian Paula D. Hunt, "Sybil Ludington: The Female Paul Revere," ran in a 2015 issue of *The New England Quarterly* and points out that Ludington never mentioned riding on behalf of the American militia even late in life when she was applying to receive government benefits as the widow of someone who'd served in the military. Numerous books published in the 1800s about women who were Revolutionary heroes failed to mention Ludington. Nor did she appear in local histories of the region. Details of her journey, including the name of her horse, were introduced, like the road markers, without evidence a century after Ludington's death, after her story had begun to gain traction in the public imagination.

Hunt's piece deftly explores why the Ludington story so appealed to the public and especially at certain points in U.S. history. It certainly is an inspiring story. She was just sixteen! What Hunt does not explicitly say but what's clear from her strong research and delivery is that the public rise and development of Ludington's ride in public life—and why we know Ludington today—has been driven and sustained by a critical proximity to Paul Revere's.

One of the early articles that raised Ludington's profile ran in 1929 in the *Putnam County Courier* under the headline "Putnam County's Feminine Paul Revere." That phrasing may have influenced another important piece of writing on Ludington, which appeared in *The Sunday Star* about a decade later. You guessed it: a poem. Here is the opening stanza of Berton Braley's Longfellow parody, "Sybil Ludington's Ride":

> Listen, my children, and you shall hear
> Of a lovely feminine Paul Revere
> Who rode an equally famous ride
> Through a different part of the countryside
> Where Sybil Ludington's name recalls
> A ride as daring as that of Paul's.

And here is the final stanza:

> Such is the legend of Sybil's ride
> To summon the men from the countryside
> A true tale, making her title clear
> As a lovely feminine Paul Revere!

Not long ago, while stumping for museum funding, Representative Carolyn Maloney of New York described Ludington as "a woman who rode longer and farther than Paul Revere." Hunt cites remarks made in the 1970s by Connecticut representative Stewart B. McKinney in which he decried "the yoke of discrimination against sex and age," remarks that were headlined "Pauline Revere." (Yes, the irony's rich.)

In the introduction to her excellent 2023 book, *Young and Restless: The Girls Who Sparked America's Revolutions,* Mattie Kahn comes to question the authenticity of Ludington's ride, but only after introducing her as someone who "outrode Paul Revere," in the way you might say that an apple out-appled an orange.

Whatever elements of Ludington's ride are or are not true, her legend carries a debt of its own: the facts and echoes of Revere's ride gave life to the extraordinary story of Sybil Ludington.

ON THE DAY I met Paul Revere III, at his Massachusetts home some sixty-eight miles from Boston's North End, he wore a white T-shirt emblazoned on the left breast with REVERE in red lettering, encircled by blue stars of the same shape and style as the stars on the U.S. flag. The back of his T-shirt read LAW OFFICES OF PAUL REVERE III "RIDING TO YOUR RESCUE" and featured a silhouette of a man galloping on horseback, a colonial-style hat on his head and the tails of his frock coat flared out behind him.

Revere III runs a solo law practice on Cape Cod, specializing in issues surrounding environmental compliance and land use development. He's in his midsixties, small, fit, and wiry, and a competitive weekend sailor. He does not ride a horse, nor does his sister, Avery.

"People ask me, 'What's it like to go through life with

the name Paul Revere?'" Revere III says. "I tell them, I don't know what it's like *not* to go through life with the name Paul Revere. I don't know what it's like to tell someone your name and *not* have them stop and stare at you like, *You're kidding*."

He looks like his namesake, in a faint way. A similar flare at the side of the nostril, same forehead, a certain crease at the side of the mouth. Revere III is in fact six generations removed—not all male descendants have been named Paul along the way. Paul Revere the Patriot (as descendants sometimes call him) was Revere III's great-great-great-great-grandfather. Revere III's great-great-great-grandfather was Joseph Warren Revere, who was born in 1777 and named for Revere's great friend who died at Bunker Hill. Revere III's grandfather was named Paul Revere, his father was Paul Revere, Jr., and Revere III named his son Paul Revere IV.

"On a family level there's a quality of Paul Revere the Patriot that has carried through," says Revere III. "It's the idea that he was comfortable with everyone, however much money or little money you had, whatever you did for a living, he gave respect and friendship. That is a big part of what I believe in and we believe in."

Revere Jr., who died in 2019, headed the Paul Revere Memorial Association for forty years, and Revere III says that he participates in public interviews and events in part to help sustain the tourism industry around Revere and the Revolutionary time in Boston. On Patriots' Day in 2009 he threw out the first pitch at the Red Sox game. The game was delayed by rain, and when his name was announced, a group of already-tanked fans behind the dugout started bellowing out to him in incredulity and delight, "It's Paul Reveah! Paul Reveah! Go get it, Reveah!"

He has some items directly passed down, including a large silver spoon that was not only smithed by Revere sometime in the late 1760s, but was also used by the family. There's a crimp in it. He has an invoice written and signed by Revere for work done in 1816. One of Revere III's great-uncles had the Copley portrait of Revere hanging in his home for years before donating it to the Museum of Fine Arts, Boston, in 1930. When Revere III met Sam Adams, also a Massachusetts lawyer, and, yes, a descendant of Samuel Adams, Revere III said, "You and I, we have some things to talk about."

Naturally, Revere III's father also had a lifetime of touched interactions, including this one: In the late 1960s, on a weekday, April 18, he was coming home from work driving along Route 2 in Lexington when he saw the lights of a police car flashing behind him. He was getting pulled over for speeding.

"License and registration, please," the officer said.

Revere handed them over. The officer took the documents and returned to his car, then sat there for what seemed to Revere a long time. Finally, the policeman came back to Revere's window and handed back the license and registration. "Okay, you can go on home," the officer said. No ticket. "There is just no way that I can go back to the station and say I gave Paul Revere a ticket for speeding in Lexington on April 18."

"It was just too good a story," Revere III says. "I always had this kind of 'Yeah, right, Dad' feeling about it. Then a few years ago I was working a case in Boston, and this other attorney came up to me and said, 'Did your dad ever get pulled over in Lexington? Because I once had a state trooper tell me this story . . .'"

IN THE LATE winter of 2024, a few months after spending time with Revere III, I arranged to climb to the steeple chamber at Old North Church. I made the arrangements with some trepidation, and a brief story may illustrate why.

Some years back I was assigned to write a story for *Sports Illustrated* about a young rock climber, Chris McNamara, who was making historic ascents of El Capitan, the gorgeous, forbidding rock face in Yosemite Park. During our time together McNamara and I drove to the top of another of Yosemite's looming cliffs and got out to walk around. Standing near the edge, thousands of feet above the valley floor, McNamara looked out over the park and was telling me about his love of climbing when he noticed I was far back from the edge, maybe twenty feet from him. "I'm sorry," I said. "I'm a little nervous to stand where you're standing."

McNamara reassured me. He said he himself had a fear of heights, and that having some fear was healthy even for a climber because it helped prevent sloppiness and unnecessary risk-taking. "One thing I did for a long time when I wanted to look out from a place like this is, I would lie down on my stomach and just move my face near to the edge," said McNamara. "You could try that."

"Okay," I said. I lay down on my stomach and immediately felt much better and more secure—but I did not come even one inch closer to the edge. I held to my spot twenty feet back, chin to the ground as we talked. I do not like heights. The steeple chamber at Old North Church, snug and with windows on all four sides, is more than 150 feet above the sidewalk below.

"If you fall and land inside the property, it's our responsibility," said Julius Hobert, the visitor experience manager at Old North Church, who was acting as my guide. "If you fall outside the property, you're on your own."

Hobert laughed and winked. Then he handed me a waiver to sign, protecting the church from liability in the event I got injured during our climb.

Getting up to the bell ringers' room was simple—two

well-maintained public staircases. From there we took another staircase, this one winding with uneven steps of unpainted wood. That brought us to the belfry, which houses the same still-active bells that Revere rang as a teenager and which Robert Newman passed en route to showing the lanterns. From here things got a little trickier.

We climbed via a series of wooden ladders—each of them with ten to twelve flat rungs, widely spaced. Each ladder rose to a trapdoor, which Hobert, leading the way, pushed open. We'd go up through the trapdoor, come to a small landing, stand for a moment, and then climb the next ladder. Around us were the church's structural essentials: thick crossbeams, rafters, support cables.

"Don't look down," Hobert advised when we were a few ladders past the belfry.

"Okay," I managed. The air was cool, and I was in shirt-sleeves, but I had begun to sweat.

"Don't look up either," he said.

Outside was dark. A bit of light shone up from the belfry below us, and some small bulbs were positioned on the walls along the way, though they were not particularly bright. From a landing you could see the steeple chamber a few stories up—to me it seemed more distant than that—and moonlight came in through the windows there. Moonlight would have been all that Newman had in 1775.

I gripped the sides of each ladder as we climbed and

tried to abide by Hobert's don't-look-up, don't-look-down guidance. He was quicker over the rungs than I was, and he would wait for me on each landing. A few more ladders up. Hobert opened the trapdoor leading to the landing that lay just below the steeple chamber. Suddenly a cold wind, continuous and whooshing, came into the space, through tall louvered windows. Wire meshing prevented pigeons from coming in, as they had during the time of Newman's ascent and of Longfellow's. I felt exposed, vulnerable, with the wind blowing around us.

"Just one more to go," Hobert said. I concentrated on the positioning of my hands and knees and I leaned into the ladder as we climbed the last steps. I closed my eyes. Hobert and I didn't talk at all. And then, suddenly, we were up! Into the steeple chamber, looking out in all directions at the cityscape around us. A broad, glittering panorama. The view was of course not at all as Newman would have seen it. Lighted offices, an indoor basketball court, a dance class in session at the Y. Tall glass and steel structures here and there. Broad rooftops planted with greenery. Farther down, cars moved and honked, along the streets.

But still, there to the west lay the graveyard at Copp's Hill, and then the downward slope and the Charles River beyond it. Across the water you could see Charlestown and the landing area where Paul Revere stepped out of his rowboat that night.

"Beautiful, right?" said Hobert, looking around. Hobert comes up to the steeple chamber from time to time, the Old North Church's unofficial escort. Many among the church staff aren't as keen to make the ascent.

We stayed there for a while, noticing things and talking about the history of the church and the way things might have happened that night. Boats floated on the river at the point where the *Somerset* had swung on her moorings. The night was clear and starry, and neither of us felt in a hurry to go down. For whatever reason, up here the height, and the vantage point with the night air coming in through opened windows, felt fine to me.

When we did go down, we went fairly quickly. I led the way so that Hobert could pull each trapdoor shut behind us. Down through the whistling wind, the landing-to-landing descent to the belfry and then to the staircases and the rooms below. We'd had a less demanding trip than Newman had ventured—better light, sturdier ladders, no lanterns draped over our necks, no British officers to be wary of—but we and he had traveled the same path.

IN JUNE OF 1775, two months after the night when Revere, Bentley, and Richardson rowed undetected past her decks, the HMS *Somerset* bombarded Patriot troops—albeit with minimal effectiveness—at the Battle of Bunker

Hill. She remained engaged as the Revolutionary War progressed, often sailing along the coast of Cape Cod, where British sailors would come ashore, disrupt business, and seize supplies. On the stormy night of November 2, 1778, the *Somerset* ran aground, wrecking against a sandbar between Truro and Provincetown. Local militia swarmed to the site and took the more than four hundred surviving seamen (dozens of others had died in the wreck) as prisoners. The locals pillaged the *Somerset*'s supplies and eventually, in a show of defiance and triumph, burned the ship to the waterline.

From time to time over the past 250 years, depending upon the season and the tides, the remains of the *Somerset* have presented themselves off the Cape Cod shore. When they appeared in 1973, the National Park Service cut away and stored huge pieces of her hull. Now when the last vestiges of the ship come to light—as they did in 2010 and 2017—they emerge as skeletal slabs of wood, barely protruding out of the sand. The larger remains, those that were taken in 1973, are housed about two miles away in an old cinder-block building that from 1950 until the mid-1990s was used as a barracks and a storage area at the now-defunct U.S. Air Force Radar Station in Truro. The station complex sits on the seaward bend of the cape, at one of its outermost points.

"There's a contention that whatever is left of the wreckage belongs to the British navy," said Bill Burke, a historian with the National Park Service, as we ran our hands along smooth parts of the salvaged hull. "But no one's asking for this."

The dark oak slabs, curved and massive, show the weathering of the ship's life, but little recent decay—even though they've never been treated or preserved. The wood is thick, heavy, solid, and without rot. "It spent about two hundred years under the sand and the water, so no oxygen got to it," says Burke. The treenails hold firmly in place, and on some of them you can make out the professional markings of a builder who three hundred years ago and an ocean away helped give life to the great ship, the ship that loomed large and black in the Charles River on the night that Paul Revere slipped past.

"I've just finished dinner and now I'm outside the house waiting for Paul Revere to ride into town," the woman said into her cell phone. It was nearly midnight on an April Sunday, the eve of Patriots' Day 2024 in Lexington, Massachusetts. Hundreds of people had gathered on the street by the Hancock-Clarke House, and when Paul Revere—an accurately garbed reenactor named Bruce Leader—did ride up, the crowd cheered loud enough that it startled Leader's horse. Leader had not ridden to Reverend Clarke's house from Boston, but rather from a church parking lot a few hundred yards down the road.

Because of highways, other roads, and all manner of modern construction, it's not practical to ride Revere's route today. You can drive it, roughly, although following the route over miles of asphalt and passing Mobil stations and Dunkin' Donuts along the way tends to mitigate the sense of being there.

You can, however, ride a bicycle on a dirt road in Minute Man Park, just west of Lexington, a stretch of about 1.8 miles from Fiske Hill to the spot where Revere, Dawes, and Prescott were captured. Signs and information placards along the way tell visitors where they are and what they are looking at. A couple of stone markers flanked by fresh British flags show the words NEAR HERE ARE BURIED BRITISH SOLDIERS. APRIL 19TH, 1775. The last miles of Revere's ride are also part of the road, Battle Road, where the Patriot militia covered the retreating redcoats, giving them ball for ball.

Many of the walkers along this path don't stop to read the placards or to take in the landmarks. It's easy, when riding your bike past a couple pushing a stroller, and a woman jogging with her dog, and a kid with his earbuds in, and an older man using a cane, to feel as if you are in any park anywhere. But if you come to this stretch at night, under a clear sky with the moon lighting the way, and if you take in the eighteenth-century homes still standing along the way and notice the boulders by the side of the road, and then see among the stands of deciduous trees the open fields and low hills, and if there is no sound from another road and no light from anywhere but above, then you can see it all, see that this is where it happened, the last miles of it, on just such a night 250 years ago: the Ride.

ACKNOWLEDGMENTS

Early reporting for this book included visits to the Paul Revere House, the seat of the Paul Revere Memorial Association and a kind of ground zero for the Ride. The house and the association operate under the leadership of executive director Nina Zannieri, who helped to situate me in Revere's world, then and now. Zannieri lent her knowledge and insight, and she steered me toward valuable resources. Among those resources: Charles "Charlie" Bahne of Cambridge and his excellent measurements of the distances traveled by Revere, William Dawes, and others on the night of April 18, 1775. Through Zannieri I met Paul Revere III, the direct descendant who fielded my questions, embraced our conversations, and gave life to his ancestral past. Paul carries the name and carries it well. The written work of scholars associated with the Paul Revere Memorial Association—in particular the work of Patrick M. Leehey and Edith Steblecki—was also of great help to the book.

At Old North Church, thank you to Jason Fishman and Catherine Matthews for opening those magnificent doors, and to Emily Spence for her time and expertise, and to Julius Hobert, a superb guide and keen observer, who still has a Monica's Mercato sub coming to him.

The book was buoyed by Bill Burke of the Cape Cod National Seashore, and the time we spent together on the Outer Cape visiting the remains of the HMS *Somerset* and then negotiating the rolling dunes to see the waters where the great ship came to an end.

Portsmouth's Fort William and Mary, long since renamed Fort Constitution, stands today where it stood then. Thank you to Elizabeth Jurgilewicz, Matthew Flanders and Doug Fletcher for sharing from their wealth of information about the fort and for allowing me to scrounge around the grounds and get a lay of the land.

Researching at the Massachusetts Historical Society was a gift rife with revelation, delivered through a conscientious staff and a remarkable collection of documents, letters, artifacts, and other material. Also highly illuminative were the troves at the New Hampshire Historical Society (thank you, Paul Friday), the Portsmouth Athenaeum (thank you, Robin Silva), the Concord Museum (thank you, Shane Clarke), and the Lexington Historical Society (thank you, Kate Criscitiello and Jesse Hilton). A salute to the staffs at the public libraries in Concord, Lincoln, and Portsmouth, and a special thanks to Jamie Jaroff at the Barrow Bookstore in Concord.

For horse sense, I turned to a good friend and good writer, Charlie Leerhsen. He led me to one expert, Ellen Harvey, who led me to another, Aarene Storms, whose knowledge and passion for the subject are, I can confirm, contagious.

A big Lexington thanks to Henry Liu for his time and know-how, and to Bruce Leader, a reenactor of high standards and with a gracious way.

At some point the path of a book, like the path of many an event in history, moves from improbable to inevitable. Now, as ever, I'm grateful for the fine counsel of my literary agent, Andrew Blauner. And I feel lucky to work with the superb George Witte at St. Martin's Press. George's excellent eye and sense of measure, among much else, greatly benefited this book. At St. Martin's, thank you also to Brigitte Dale, Joseph Rinaldi, Mac Nicholas, Sara Beth Haring, and to Steve Boldt for his fine copyediting and fact-checking.

From backstage, a big thanks to David Bauer for reading some early pages and lending his typically sage advice.

To an American woman, Kathrin Perutz (who first read me Longfellow's verse), and to an Englishman, Michael Studdert-Kennedy (who always asked the next good question), thank you for hanging the lanterns, for showing me a way.

To Sonya, for her voice and young wisdom, and to Maya, who inspires me within these pages and without: thank you for being just as you are. Absent the love, patience, and encouragement of Amy Levine-Kennedy, this book would not have been written. Thank you for all of it and so much more.

SELECTED BIBLIOGRAPHY

Books

Adams, Nathaniel. *Annals of Portsmouth: Comprising a Period of Two Hundred Years from the First Settlement of the Town; with Biographical Sketches of a Few of the Most Respectable Inhabitants.* Portsmouth, N.H.: C. Norris, 1825.

Albee, John. *New Castle Historic and Picturesque.* Portsmouth, N.H.: Randall, 1974.

Alden, John Richard. *General Gage in America, Being Principally a History of His Role in the American Revolution.* Baton Rouge: Louisiana State University Press, 1948.

Barrett, Carrie Rebora. *John Singleton Copley in America.* New York: Metropolitan Museum of Art; Harry N. Abrams, 1995.

Basbanes, Nicholas A. *Cross of Snow: A Life of Henry Wadsworth Longfellow.* New York: Knopf, 2020.

Bayley, Frank W. *The Life and Works of John Singleton Copley (Founded on the Work of Augustus Thorndike Perkins).* London: Forgotten, 2016.

Beilock, Sian. *Choke: What the Secrets of the Brain Reveal About Getting It Right When You Have To.* New York: Atria, 2010.

Bell, J. L. *The Road to Concord: How Four Stolen Cannon Ignited the Revolutionary War.* Yardley, Pa.: Westholme, 2016.

Billias, George. *General John Glover and His Marblehead Marines.* New York: Henry Holt, 1960.

Black, Jeremy. *George III: America's Last King.* New Haven, Conn.: Yale University Press, 2006.

Boston and the Sea: The Development of a Colonial Seaport. Boston: Paul Revere Memorial Association, 1985.

Brewster, Charles W. *Rambles About Portsmouth, First Series: Sketches of Persons, Localities and Incidents of Two Centuries.* Portsmouth, N.H.: Lewis W. Brewster, 1873.

Brigham, Clarence, S. *Paul Revere's Engravings.* New York: Atheneum, 1969.

Brown, Abram English. *History of the Town of Bedford, Middlesex County, Massachusetts; Earliest Settlement to the Year of Our Lord 1891.* Bedford, Mass.: published by the author, 1891.

Butterfield, L. H. *The Diary and Autobiography of John Adams.* Vol. 2. Cambridge, Mass.: Belknap Press of Harvard University Press, 1961.

Calhoun, Charles C. *Longfellow: A Rediscovered Life.* Boston: Beacon Press, 2004.

Carter, Clarence Edwin, ed. *The Correspondence of General Thomas Gage.* 2 vols. Hamden, Conn.: Archon Books, 1969.

Cary, John. *Joseph Warren: Physician, Politician, Patriot.* Urbana: University of Illinois Press, 1961.

Clark, William Bell, ed. *Naval Documents of the American Revolution.* Vol. 1. Washington, D.C.: U.S. Navy Department, 1964.

Clarke, Jonas. *The Battle of Lexington: A Sermon and Eyewitness Narrative.* Ventura, Calif.: Nordskog, 2007.

Club of Odd Volumes. *Late News of the Excursion and Ravages of the King's Troops on the Nineteenth of April 1775. As Set Forth in the Narratives of Lieut. William Sutherland of His Majesty's 38th Regiment of Foot and of Richard Pope of the 47th Regiment.* Cambridge, Mass.: Press at Harvard College, 1927.

Coburn, Frank Warren. *The Battle of April 19, 1775, in Lexington, Concord, Lincoln, Arlington, Cambridge, Somerville and Charlestown, Massachusetts.* Lexington, Mass.: published by the author, 1912.

Coldham, Peter Wilson. *American Migrations, 1765–1799.* Baltimore, Md.: Genealogical Publishing, 2000.

Cushing, Harry Alonzo, ed. *Writings of Samuel Adams.* Vols. 2–4. New York: G. P. Putnam's Sons, 1906.

Daughan, George C. *Lexington and Concord: The Battle Heard Round the World.* New York: W. W. Norton, 2018.

Dawes, C. Burr. *William Dawes: First Rider for Revolution.* Newark, Ohio: Historic Gardens Press, 1976.

Dexter, Franklin Bowditch. *The Literary Diary of Ezra Stiles.* Vol. 1. New York: Charles Scribner's Sons, 1901.

Di Spigna, Christian. *Founding Martyr: The Life and Death of Dr. Joseph Warren, the American Revolution's Lost Hero.* New York: Crown, 2018.

Drake, Francis S. *Tea Leaves.* Independently published from works in the public domain, 2012.

Drake, Francis Samuel. *The Town of Roxbury: Its Memorable Persons and Places, Its History and Antiquities, with Numerous Illustrations of Its Old Landmarks and Noted Personages.* Roxbury, Mass.: published by the author, 1878.

Drake, Samuel Adams. *Old Landmarks and Historic Personages of Boston.* Rutland, Vt.: Charles E. Tuttle, 1971.

Ensign, William. *Some Descendants of Stephen Lincoln of Wymondham, England, Edward Larkin from England, Thomas Oliver of Bristol, England, Michael Pearce of London, England, Robert Wheaton of Swansea, Wales, George Burrill of Boston, England, John Porter of Dorset, England, John Ayer of Norwich, England, and Notes of Related Families.* Lincoln, Mass.: printed for the author, 1930.

Ferris, Mary Walton. *Dawes-Gates Ancestral Lines.* Vol. 1. Chicago: Cuneo Press, 1943.

Fischer, David Hackett. *Paul Revere's Ride.* New York: Oxford University Press, 1994.

Forbes, Esther. *Paul Revere and the World He Lived In.* New York: Houghton Mifflin, 1942.

Fowler, William M., Jr. *The Baron of Beacon Hill: A Biography of John Hancock.* Boston: Houghton Mifflin, 1980.

Fradin, Dennis. *Samuel Adams: The Father of American Independence.* New York: Clarion Books, 1998.

French, Allen. *General Gage's Informers.* New York: Greenwood, 1968.

Frothingham, Richard. *History of the Siege of Boston, and the Battles of Lexington, Concord and Bunker Hill. Also, an account of Bunker Hill Monument.* Boston: Little, Brown, 1873.

Galvin, Major John R. *The Minute Men: A Compact History of the Defenders of the American Colonies, 1645–1775.* New York: Hawthorn Books, 1967.

Gettemy, Charles Ferris. *The True Story of Paul Revere: His Mid-*

night Ride, His Arrest and Court-Martial, His Useful Public Services. Boston: Little, Brown, 1906.

Gibson, Majorie Hubbell. *H.M.S. Somerset, 1746–1778: The Life and Times of an Eighteenth Century British Man-o-War and Her Impact on North America*. Cotuit, Mass.: Abbey Gate House, 1992.

Gladwell, Malcolm. *The Tipping Point: How Little Things Can Make a Big Difference*. Boston: Little, Brown, 2000.

Goodell, Abner Cheney. *The Trial and Execution, for Petit Treason, of Mark and Phillis*. Cambridge, Mass.: John Wilson & Son, 1883.

Goss, Elbridge Henry. *The Life of Colonel Paul Revere*. Boston: Howard W. Spurr, 1898.

Grant, Louise. *The Fort & the Flag*, Hanover, N.H.: Regional Center for Educational Training, 1977.

Green, Samuel Abbott. *An Account of Percival and Ellen Green and Some of Their Descendants*. Groton, Mass.: privately printed, 1876.

Greenburg, Michael M. *The Court-Martial of Paul Revere*. Lebanon, N.H.: University of New England Press, 2014.

Greene, Lorenzo Johnston. *The Negro in Colonial New England, 1620–1776*. Port Washington, N.Y.: Kennikat, 1966.

Gross, Robert A. *The Minutemen and Their World*. New York: Farrar, Straus & Giroux, 1976.

Grossman, Nancy W. *The Placenames of Portsmouth*. Portsmouth N.H.: Backchannel Press, 2011.

Hardesty, Jared Ross. *Black Lives, Native Lands, White Worlds: A History of Slavery in New England*. Amherst, Mass.: Bright Leaf, 2019.

———. *Unfreedom: Slavery and Dependence in Eighteenth-Century Boston*. New York: New York University Press, 2016.

Hersey, Frank Wilson Cheney. *Heroes of the Battle Road.* Boston: privately printed, 1930.

Holland, Henry Ware. *William Dawes and His Ride with Paul Revere.* Boston: John Wilson & Son, 1878.

Hurd, D. Hamilton. *History of Middlesex County, Massachusetts with Biographical Sketches on Many of Its Pioneers and Prominent Men.* 2 vols. Philadelphia: J. W. Lewis, 1890.

Kamensky, Jane. *A Revolution in Color: The World of John Singleton Copley.* New York: W. W. Norton, 2016.

Kollen, Richard P. *The Patriot Parson of Lexington, Massachusetts: Reverend Jonas Clarke and the American Revolution.* Charleston, S.C.: History Press, 2016.

Larson, Edward J. *American Inheritance: Liberty and Slavery in the Birth of a Nation, 1765–1795.* New York: W. W. Norton, 2023.

Leehey, Patrick M. *What Was the Name of Paul Revere's Horse?* Boston: Paul Revere Memorial Association, 2019.

Leerhsen, Charles. *Crazy Good: The True Story of Dan Patch, the Most Famous Horse in America.* New York: Simon & Schuster, 2008.

Malcolm, Joyce Lee. *The Scene of the Battle, 1775. Historic Grounds Report.* USA: Division of Cultural Resources, North Atlantic Regional Office, National Park Service, U.S. Department of the Interior, 1985.

Martello, Robert. *Midnight Ride, Industrial Dawn: Paul Revere and the Growth of American Enterprise.* Baltimore, Md: Johns Hopkins University Press, 2010.

May, Samuel. *Memoir of Col. Joseph May, 1760–1841.* Boston: David Claff & Son, 1873.

Middlekauff, Robert. *The Glorious Cause: The American Revolution, 1763–1789.* New York: Oxford University Press, 2005.

Miller, Joel J. *The Revolutionary Paul Revere.* Nashville, Tenn.: Thomas Nelson, 2010.

Mitchell, Patricia B. *Revolutionary Recipes: Colonial Food, Lore, & More.* Virginia: Patricia B. Mitchell, 1988.

O'Brien, Harriet E. *Paul Revere's Own Story.* USA: Perry Walton, 1929.

O'Donnell, Patrick K. *The Indispensables: The Diverse Soldier-Mariners Who Shaped the Country, Formed the Navy and Rowed Washington Across the Delaware.* New York: Atlantic Monthly Press, 2021.

Phillips, James Duncan. *Salem in the Eighteenth Century,* New York: Houghton Mifflin, 1937.

Phinney, Elias. *History of the Battle of Lexington on the Morning of April 19, 1775.* Boston: Phelps & Farnham, 1825.

Raphael, Ray. *A People's History of the American Revolution.* New York: New Press, 2001.

Richmond, Robert P. *The Powder Alarm.* New York: Auerbach, 1971.

Ripley, Elizabeth. *Copley: A Biography.* Philadelphia: Lippincott, 1967.

Sewall, Samuel, Charles Chauncey Sewall, George Mather Champney, and Samuel Thompson. *The History of Woburn, Middlesex County, Mass.* Boston: Wiggin and Lunt, 1868.

Sheets, Robert Newman. *Robert Newman: His Life and Letters.* Denver, Colo.: Newman Family Society, 1975.

———. *Robert Newman, the Life and Times of the Sexton Who April 18, 1775, Held Two Lanterns Aloft in Christ Church Steeple, Boston.* Denver, Colo.: Newman Family Society, 1975.

Small, Mary Jane. *Four Dentists & a Musician.* New Harbor, Maine: MJ Small Books, 2002.

Spurr, Howard W. *The Paul Revere Album.* Boston: Howard W. Spurr Coffee Co., 1897.

Stabler, Lois K., ed. *Very Poor and of a Lo Make: The Journal of Abner Sanger.* Portsmouth, N.H.: Peter E. Randall, 1986.

Stackpole, Everett S., Lucien Thompson, and Winthrop W. Meserve. *History of the Town of Durham, New Hampshire.* Somersworth, N.H.: New England History Press, 1973.

Steblecki, Edith J. *Paul Revere and Freemasonry.* Boston: Paul Revere Memorial Association, 1985.

Stickney, Edward and Evelynn. *The Bells of Paul Revere, His Sons, and Grandsons.* Revised and edited by Patrick M. Leehey. Boston: Paul Revere Memorial Association, 2022.

Stoll, Ira. *Samuel Adams: A Life.* New York: Free Press, 2008.

Thwing, Annie Haven. *The Crooked & Narrow Streets of the Town of Boston. 1630–1822.* Boston: Marshall Jones, 1920.

Ticknor, Caroline. *The "Old North" Signal-Lights, 1723–1923.* Boston: Riverside Press Cambridge, 1923.

Triber, Jayne E. *A True Republican: The Life of Paul Revere.* Amherst: University of Massachusetts Press, 1998.

Tully, Richard M. *A Brief Discourse on Eighteenth Century Games.* Baraboo, Wis.: Ballindalloch Press, 2006.

Unger, Harlow Giles. *John Hancock: Merchant King and American Patriot.* New York: John Wiley & Sons, 2000.

Webster, Mary Phillipe, and Charles R. Morris. *The Story of the Suffolk Resolves.* Milton, Mass.: Milton Historical Society, 1973.

Wheildon, William W. *Curiosities of History: Boston, September Seventeenth, 1630–1880.* Boston: Lee & Shephard, 1880.

———. *Paul Revere's Signal Lanterns.* Concord, Mass.: author's private printing office, 1878.

Wild, Helen Tilden. *Medford in the Revolution: Military History of Medford, Massachusetts, 1765–1783*. Medford, Mass.: J. C. Miller, Jr., Printer, 1903.

Zabin, Serena. *The Boston Massacre: A Family History*. New York: Houghton Mifflin, 2020.

Articles

Akroyd, Elizabeth Rhoades. "Note on the Raids on Fort William and Mary." *Historical New Hampshire* 32, No. 3 (Fall 1977).

Bahne, Charles. "One Hundred and Fifty Years of 'Paul Revere's Ride'—a Sesquicentennial Observation." *Revere House Gazette* 99 (Summer 2010).

Balun, Jessica. "Sybil Luddington—a Female Paul Revere?" *Revere House Gazette* 54 (Spring 1999).

Batchelden, Samuel Francis. "Harvard Hospital-Surgeons of 1775: A Study in the Medical History of the American Revolution." As read before the Harvard Medical Society, January 6, 1920.

Beck, Derek W. "Dr. Joseph Warren's Informant." *Journal of the American Revolution*, 2014.

Bell, J. L. Various entries. *Boston 1775* (blog). https://boston1775.blogspot.com/.

Bennett, Deb. "Horses of the American Colonies." *Equus* 468 (September 2016).

Boaz, Thomas. "Major John Pitcairn and the British Marines in Boston." Massachusetts Historical Society, 1991.

Bohy, Joel. "A Portrait Painted by Paul Revere and a Moment in American History." *Bonhams Skinner*, February 14, 2014.

Brown, G. W. "Sketch of the Life of Solomon Brown." Lexington Historical Society, proceedings read May 12, 1891.

Chase, Theodore. "The Attack on Fort William and Mary." *Historical New Hampshire* 18, No. 1 (April 1963).

Clark, Emily Jeannine. "'Their Negro Nanny Was with Child by a White Man': Gossip, Sex, and Slavery in an Eighteenth-Century New England Town." *William and Mary Quarterly,* October 2022.

Comstock, William O. "Four Mounted Messengers of the Revolution." *Riverdale Press* (Brookline, Mass.), 1913.

Doane, Charles. "Paul Revere's Signal: Letter from John Lee Watson." *Proceedings of the Massachusetts Historical Society* 15 (1876–77).

Drighton, Ray. "Portsmouth Men Attacked British in Fort Constitution 175 Years Ago." *Portsmouth Herald,* December 13, 1949.

Eastman, Anne and Charles W., Jr. "All This Battle Needs Is a Poet." *Historical New Hampshire* 18, No. 1 (April 1963).

———. "The Final Straws. New Hampshire on the Morning of Revolution: The Attack on Fort William and Mary." *New Hampshire Profiles,* December 1974.

Endicott, Charles M. "Leslie's Retreat at the North Bridge in Salem." *Proceedings of the Essex Institute,* 1856.

Feldscher, Karen. "Recalling Joseph Warren—Physician, Revolutionary, Leader." Harvard T. H. Chan School of Public Health, March 23, 2012.

Fletcher, Ron. "Who's Buried in Dawes's Tomb?" *Boston Globe,* February 25, 2007.

Flood, Peter. "A Week in December: Paul Revere's Secret Mission to New Hampshire." *Revere House Gazette* 114 (Spring 2011). Also original manuscript, courtesy New Hampshire Historical Society.

Gioia, Dana. "Henry Wadsworth Longfellow: On 'Paul Revere's Ride,'" danagioia.com. From *An Introduction to Poetry*

/ *Columbia History of Poetry*. Upper Saddle River, N.J.: Pearson, 2009.

Gleason, Hall. "Capt. Isaac Hall." Read before the Medford Historical Society, 1905.

Gopnik, Adam. "How Samuel Adams Helped Ferment a Revolution." *New Yorker,* October 31, 2022.

Hafner, Donald. "First Blood Shed in the Revolution: The Tale of Josiah Nelson on April 19, 1775." Boston College University Library, 2015.

"Historic Fort Yields Artifacts." *Beachcomber,* August 14, 1969.

"History of Boston Harbor." Water Resources Authority, Massachusetts.

Hsiung, David C. "Food, Fuel, and the New England Environment in the War for Independence, 1775–1776." *New England Quarterly* 80, No. 4 (December 2007).

Hunt, Paula D. "Sybil Ludington, the Female Paul Revere: The Making of a Revolutionary War Heroine." *New England Quarterly* 88, No. 2 (June 2015).

Ingmire, Bruce E. "Paul Revere, the Spy Rides to Portsmouth." Portsmouth Athenaeum.

Kehr, Thomas F. "The Seizure of His Majesty's Fort William and Mary at New Castle, New Hampshire, December 14–15, 1774." Portsmouth Athenaeum. ppolinks.com /athenaeum/.

Klein, Christopher. "The Midday Ride of Paul Revere" *Smithsonian Magazine,* December 12, 2011.

Lasser, Ethan W. "Selling Silver: The Business of Copley's *Paul Revere.*" *American Art* 26, No. 3 (2012).

Lepore, Jill. "Paul Revere's Ride Against Slavery." *New York Times,* December 18, 2010.

———. "'Paul Revere's Ride': Awakening Abolitionists." *American Educator,* summer 2011.

MacQuarrie, Brian. "Paul Revere's Legacy Gallops On: Family Carries Weight and Honor of the Past into the Present." *Boston Globe,* December 1, 2019.

Mandrey, Dr. William. "Aroused Patriots Raid Portsmouth Fort, Seize Powder for Bunker Hill." *Portsmouth Herald,* December 13, 1949.

Martello, Robert. "The Last Ride of Paul Revere: Patriotism and Innovation in Early American Manufacturing." *Revere House Gazette* 105 (Winter 2011).

McGovern, Jerry. "McKibben Explores Big Questions in Memoir." *Adirondack Daily Enterprise,* March 13, 2024.

"Mehitable May Dawes: Wife of American Patriot William Dawes Jr." *Women in the American Revolution.* womenhistoryblog.com.

Miles, Lion G. "The True Story of Bissell's Ride in 1775." iBerkshires.com, July 21, 2004.

"The Narragansett Pacer: The Lost Horse of the New England Colonies." New England Historical Society. newengland historicalsociety.com.

Nola, Mike F. "Paul Revere and Forensic Dentistry." *Military Medicine* 181 (July 2016).

Page, Elwin L. "What Happened to the King's Powder?" *Historical New Hampshire* 19, No. 2 (Summer 1964).

Parsons, Charles L. "The Capture of Fort William and Mary, December 14 and 15, 1774." *Proceedings of the New Hampshire Historical Society,* June 4, 1899.

Pencak, William. "Dawes, William," In *American National Biography Online.* Oxford University Press, 2000.

Poole, Bill. "Nathan Munroe: A Brief Biography." lexington minutemen.com, 2018

Resistance, Kira. "New Apostolic Reformation Prophet Calls Abby Abildness the Paul Revere of Pennsylvania." *Bucks County Beacon,* February 5, 2024.

Revere, Paul. "Deposition: Corrected Copy." Massachusetts Historical Society.

———. "Deposition: Draft." Massachusetts Historical Society.

———. "Letter from Col. Paul Revere." Massachusetts Historical Society, January 1, 1798.

Rodwin, Nina. "Mark Hung in Chains: Slavery & Paul Revere's Midnight Ride." Paul Revere House, 2021.

Rothenberg, Winifred B. "The Market and Massachusetts Farmers, 1750–1855." *Journal of Economic History* 41 (June 1981).

Sanderson, Phil. "Ft. William & Mary Seized Just 180 Years Ago." *New Hampshire Sunday News,* December 12, 1954.

———. "Paul Revere's N.H. Ride." *Boston Sunday Globe,* December 12, 1954.

Saunders, Janet McGee. "Revere Bill to City Up for Bid." *Portsmouth Herald,* September 25, 1996.

Scott, Kenneth. "Colonial Innkeepers of New Hampshire." *Historical New Hampshire* 19, No. 1 (Spring 1964).

Stossel, Sage. "Paul Revere's Ride." *Atlantic,* November 23, 2011.

Tanner, Virginia. "A Pageant of Portsmouth: In Celebration of the Tercentenary of the First Settlement in New Hampshire, Spring 1623." Concord, N.H.: Rumford Press, 1923.

Thompson, Thomas C. "The Life Course and Labor of a Colonial Farmer." *Historical New Hampshire* 40, Nos. 3 & 4 (Fall/Winter 1985).

Viets, Henry R. "Samuel Prescott and His Midnight Ride." *New England Journal of Medicine,* April 19, 1956.

"Voices of the Revolution: The Five Riders." ConstitutionFacts .com.

Walsh, James Leslie. "Friend of Government or Damned Tory: The Creation of the Loyalist Identity in Revolutionary New Hampshire, 1774–1784." University of New Hampshire Scholars' Repository Doctoral Dissertations Student Scholarship, Fall 1996.

Warren, Joseph. "Oration Delivered at Boston, March 5, 1772."

Watson, John Lee. "Paul Revere's Signal." *Boston Daily Advertiser,* July 1876.

Wentworth, John. "A Proclamation by the Governor." Council-Chamber, Portsmouth, December 26, 1774.

"When Paul Revere Rode to New Hampshire." New England Historical Society, 2021.

Whiting, Gloria McMahon. "Power, Patriarchy and Provision: African Families Negotiate Gender and Slavery in New England." *Journal of American History,* December 2016.

Wilderson, Paul. "The Raids on Fort William and Mary: Some New Evidence." *Historical New Hampshire* 30, No. 3 (Fall 1975).

Wilderson, Paul W., III. "John Wentworth's Narrative of the Raids on Fort William and Mary." *Historical New Hampshire* 32, No. 4 (Winter 1977).

Yates, Edgar. "Suffolk Resolves: Paul Revere's Six-Day Ride." *Boston Herald,* April 11, 1926; and full text to Massachusetts Historical Society.

Zellner, Carl. "'The Opposite Shore': Charlestown's Role in Paul Revere's Ride." *Revere House Gazette* 55 (Summer 1999).

Zielinski, Adam E. "A Glimpse at Everyday Life in the New England Colonies, 1763–1774." American Battlefield Trust, November 16, 2020.

Websites, Documents, and Miscellany

American Battlefield Trust, www.battlefields.org

American History Central, https://www.americanhistorycentral.com/

ATX Fine Arts, www.atxfinearts.com

Boston Gazette and Country Journal, January 1, 1770

Boston 1775 by J. L. Bell, boston1775.blogspot.com

Brochure, Antiracism Committee of Fallen Church, Unitarian Universalist, 2022

Buckman Tavern, signs, plaques, and other written displays

Cambridge Historical Society, historycambridge.org

Christie's, https://www.christies.com/en/lot/lot-3886728

Descendants of William Dawes Who Rode Association, wmdawes.org/ride.html

Document: John Hancock's Boston Massacre Oration, March 5, 1774

Documents and Records, Province of New Hampshire, letter: Captain John Cochran to Governor John Wentworth, December 14, 1774

Documents and Records, Province of New Hampshire, letters: Governor John Wentworth to General Thomas Gage, December 14, 1774, and December 16, 1774

Documents and Records, Province of New Hampshire, letters, various: July 6, 1774, to January 18, 1775

Extracts from Revolutionary Documents, Massachusetts Historical Society

Historyoflamps.com

Houghton Library

Journal of the Company of Military Historians

Lexington Minute Men, www.lexingtonminutemen.com/nathan-munroe.html

Library of Congress, document: "The Trial and Execution, for Petit Treason, of Mark and Phillis"

Maine Historical Society, https://www.hwlongfellow.org/works_paul_reveres_ride.shtml

Man vs. History. Paul Revere's Ride, History Channel, 2021

Maryland Gazette, September 11, 1755

Massachusetts Historical Society, www.masshist.org

Mass.gov

Metropolitan Museum of New York, www.metmuseum.org

Milton Historical Society

Museum of Fine Arts, Boston, www.mfa.com

New York Times, April 5 and April 6, 1860

Norman B. Leventhal Map & Education Center at the Boston Public Library, Digital Collections, https://collections.leventhalmap.org/search/commonwealth:q524mv160

Old North Church, www.oldnorth.com

Old South Church, www.oldsouth.org

Paul Revere House, paulreverehouse.org

Revere House radio podcast

Seacoast Region newsletter, week of January 7–13, 1972

Smithsonian Museum, www.si.edu

Supplement to the *Massachusetts Gazette,* September 15, 1774

Testimony: "The Last and Dying Words of Mark, Aged About 30 Years," from the Massachusetts Historical Society

Wickedlocal.com

INDEX

Page numbers in *italics* refer to illustrations.

ABOUT THE AUTHOR

Amy Levine-Kennedy

KOSTYA KENNEDY is the Editor in Chief of Premium Publishing at Dotdash Meredith. A former Senior Writer and Editor at *Sports Illustrated,* he is the author of *True: The Four Seasons of Jackie Robinson* as well as the *New York Times* bestsellers *56: Joe DiMaggio and the Last Magic Number in Sports* and *Pete Rose: An American Dilemma.* All three books won the CASEY Award for Best Baseball Book of the Year. He has taught at Columbia and New York University, and he lives in Westchester County, New York.

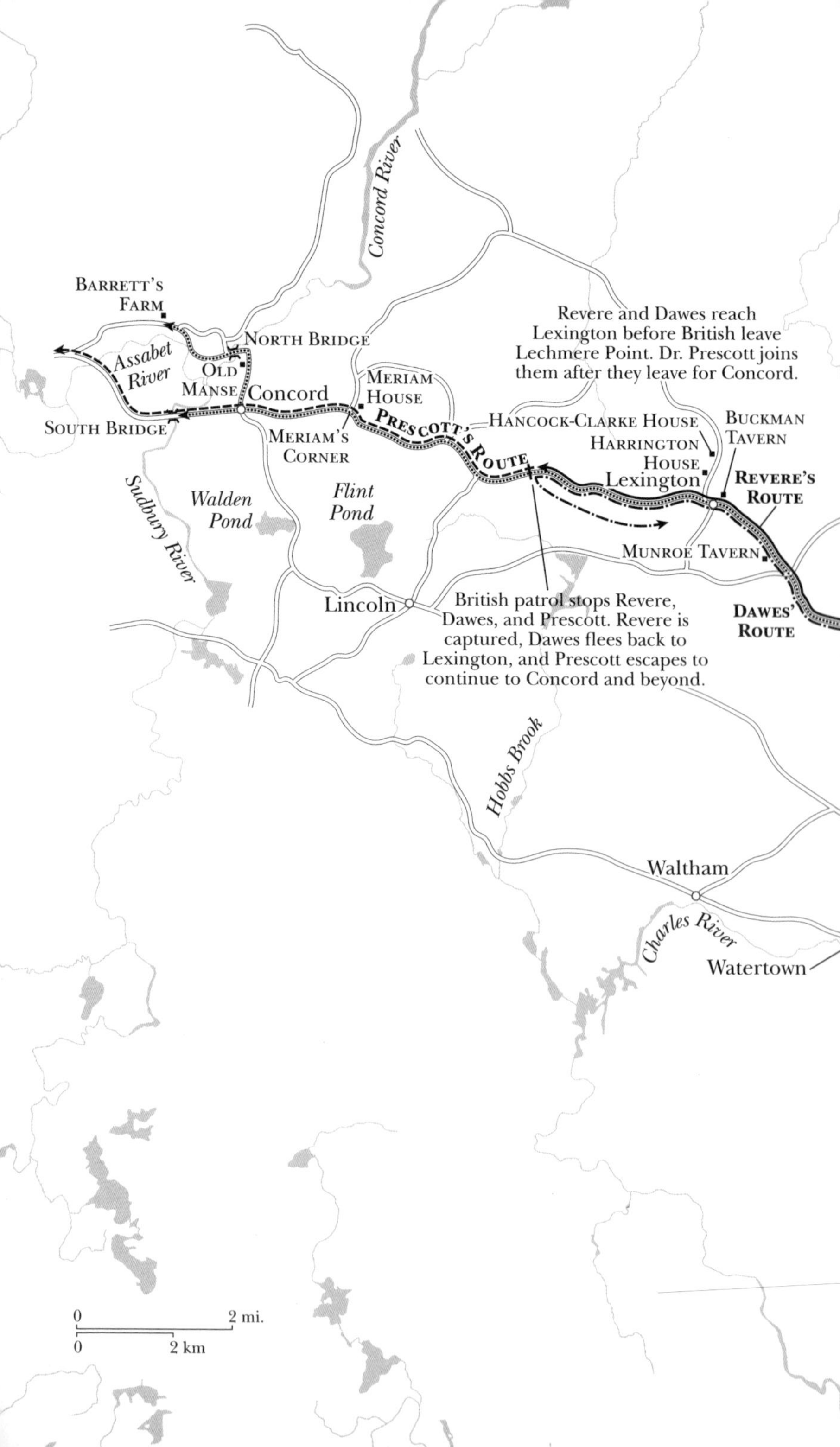
Concord River
Barrett's Farm
Assabet River
North Bridge
Old Manse
Concord
South Bridge
Meriam House
Meriam's Corner
Prescott's Route
Hancock-Clarke House
Harrington House
Buckman Tavern
Lexington
Revere's Route
Revere and Dawes reach Lexington before British leave Lechmere Point. Dr. Prescott joins them after they leave for Concord.
Sudbury River
Walden Pond
Flint Pond
Munroe Tavern
Lincoln
British patrol stops Revere, Dawes, and Prescott. Revere is captured, Dawes flees back to Lexington, and Prescott escapes to continue to Concord and beyond.
Dawes' Route
Hobbs Brook
Waltham
Charles River
Watertown
0
2 mi.
0
2 km